I Think Not Enough, Then Too Much

I talk to myself. I assume I am not alone in this, but sometimes it seems disturbing. It seems to occur either when I am trying to find something in the aisles to purchase or when you hear or read something knowing you have a differing opinion.

Although I use the computer to read articles and the like, I also receive The Wall Street Journal. Since my departure of my previous profession, I have limited myself to the weekend edition. It is enough. I still like the "feel" of the paper (although some of you younger ones probably don't know what a newspaper looks like). Anyway, one day the delivery person left The New York Times instead the WSJ. Since I will occasionally switch channels on the TV to see other views, I thought of this occurrence as another way to "study one's literary adversary", so to speak.

I rambled through the articles (saw the topics relating to Democrats more so than Republicans and others… could have just been that day). One article struck me as interesting since I am in direct conflict with its ideas. Keynesian economics, as it goes by at times, is a sort of basic thought that you can SPEND your way out of your economic blight through channeling of funds to ward off a worsening economic time (like now) in the hopes that the spending will stimulate growth. As a party of one, I do not agree with this ideology.

You want government spending to make up for shortfall in private sector demand? Create jobs that shouldn't be created, which adds more paperwork.

Just what we need, more regulations to the already encumbering regulatory environment. No wonder we stifle growth. There seems to be more of a divide in this philosophy of late between those who still think versus those who formally believed this was the way out of the economic slow down.

Could it be, once again, that politicians are afraid of losing their jobs, you know those "temporary", non-self serving positions which are supposed to represent their constituents? What a sham or shame if you like. At a time when other countries are realizing the madness of excessive deficit spending, we take their old approach? Taking "sensible actions" was the phrase mentioned…by whose standards do we judge what sensible actions are or whose lives it really touches?

I do not have any letters after my name, nor do I have a talk or anchor station on a news show to influence the opinions of others, henceforth these babblings are to the few who stumble on to these words. As an example, while some people will see some tax cuts this year, that is the cover for what is about to come.

Do you see what happens? I read some articles, start thinking about them, then start talking to myself, and voila!!...on paper again!!

Tao

I have had a "teapartyish" association branded upon me. I am not quite certain what it means because most of us have different parts associated with different ideologies. We are all different at different moments in life's pathways. It depends on how much skin one has in the game at the time.

If I had to label it at this moment, call it a Tao of Jeet Kun Do moment. With thanks to my reading of the late Mr. Bruce Lee, you can look it up if you wish. Basically, with a set of belief or beliefs, over periods of time you adhere to other ideas which may seem incoherent, baseless or just plain lack merit to others, but can and usually do change over time. Sometimes these interpretations can be made rather quickly, which is why they may be baseless. Anyway, my deep, deep thought moment is beginning to pass.

What's a Tape Recorder?

So I get up sometime in the middle of the night to use the bathroom and get any idea on some burning issue. I get back to bed, and I think K's stirring so I say "coffee" (this is the well known international code for "it's time to get up"). She says "go back to sleep". She can do that real good in no time at all. I do not share that ability. But just before she begins to "light out" again, she says, "I'm going to go out and buy you a tape recorder". I mean what the hell's a "tape" recorder anyway? Maybe there aren't enough young folks reading these passages to know. I used to have one in my business career. Once it's on the car seat, it almost begs to be used, and then you get no ideas and you miss the pen and pad. You can also use the vernacular "tape recorder" in such sayings as "honey, did you remember to TAPE the latest "Rescue Me" episode (in case you didn't auto save it). Come on, you know you've said it.

Illegal's Out the Prison Door

So what's your take on this matter? I wasn't going to use this at this time, but since this is still before elections, I find it interesting that immigration lawyers from Washington state to Texas to New York are celebrating mass releases of folks here illegally a couple of weeks prior to the elections. Gotta' make sure the these folks know who's responsible for letting them out now, so you go park yourself right by that ol' polling center, and don't you worry, no on there's gonna' stop you from voting (as long as your voting for the right people. Oh, and make sure your friends and family know what names to vote on as well. Now there's some real intelligent voting for you. No need to have any knowledge of any issues (i.e. politicians on health care). You just vote and all that free medical indigent care, schooling and lunches are coming your way...another farce. Most of the deficits facing some states today (any you know which ones they are) are primarily due to this situation.

What's In a Fortune Cookie?

Read an article today about the history of the Chinese stock and capital markets. It's been around longer than some might think. Starting in the mid 1800's, it seems history can do a lot about repeating itself even there. Booms in shipping, real estate, then rubber plantation booms, each followed by their inevitable bust. When the communists came into power after World War II, they tried to reestablish the markets, only to find capitalism wouldn't work for them.

It was noted in this country we couldn't conceive the notion of a government appointing the heads of our flagship concerns. I thought that's what we did with General Motors. I agree it shouldn't have been done for the very reason we don't want government appointing folks to these positions. They couldn't make money running a lemonade stand. You want a large order of fries with that fortune cookie?

Will that be Scotch or Bourbon with Your Vote?

Heard an interesting story in the news this morning about what may be going on in Nevada. It seems Clarke County (the main voting county population wise) is experiencing some votes already cast for a certain member of congress in advance. Isn't that nice? Hey, why bother having these old folks worry about what "chad" to punch when hey; it can be done for you without worry. Oh, and as long as you're hungry and thirsty while in line, have a "snack and Jack" while you wait. Incredible!!!

Signs! Signs! Everywhere Are Signs

In my little excursion around town this morning, I did not notice as many as it seemed last week. I am speaking of the voting kind, in case you did not guess. Maybe folks are getting more tired a little earlier of seeing them. I can't say I blame them. I mean, how much of a difference does it make to your voting decisions to see signs around that support or oppose your opinions? Maybe it's just nice to see who supports (or opposes) your cause? I don't know. It would seem you could make the decisions pretty much the same way whether these plastic and/or cardboard items were staring you in the face or otherwise. The printing companies are going to hate me for this one.

You Think You Should Still Live Where?

I wonder how many folks have been wrongly thrown out of their homes due to this ongoing real estate fiasco. I suspect not as many as we might think. I also suspect those that have been removed are many months behind in the mortgage they shouldn't have signed in the first place. You may have previously noticed I am big on throwing out the highs and the lows of things. I say this because banks and their loan procedures, whether in the implementation of the loan or foreclosure process, have been at fault as well. When the smoke clears, you a left with a lot of people who just should have known better. This may offend some, and like I said, I am moving to the side of those grievously affected unfairly and lending institutions that did blatantly violate the "oath" of their business. It has just become too easy to blame others.

November 4, 2010 – I make Print

Yesterday I was informed my first "Diary" finally made it to print. Now I can join the other minions in the flock hoping at least four copies are bought.

I find so many topics and subtopics to think and write about, so what do I think about at 5 AM this morning? A song called "Go Away, Little Girl" by Steve Lawrence. ..And I know the words!! Spooky, ain't it? The song has been done by others, but I seem to remember that version. Not even a fan, especially after you'd review my genre.

Elections-Phooey!!

Another voting season over and none too soon. It seems to get more cynical and personal attack wise every year or two, depending to on the severity of the positions up for grabs. The economy, jobs, healthcare and immigration...speaking of healthcare, I heard an organization called the National Coordination for Health Information Technology. Assuming I heard that correctly, what the hell is this? Another way to gather information about how many Big Mac's you've been eating?

Like many of our generation and before, we did not grow up on this type of food, but kids and grandkids beware. Your offspring's going to have to deal with these issues, because the government knows how to raise your kids better than you.

Crumbling Wall Street

I wonder why so many folks seem to point to Wall Street as the only or main source of the financial meltdown. They did it, and if they did the primary damage, it's only because they sold their souls to the government and got bailed out by them. In other words no matter how much risk they take, they don't ever lose (i.e. the "no skin in the game" feature) and that's nice for them.

You see famous folks crying about their losses in the market and sue their brokerage houses over it. Again, if the brokerage that took the risk had no justification or authorization to do so, they may have a case. It seems it's just mostly people who thought they had a right to make bigger returns than the rank in file, and when the returns did not pan out, they sue. Tell me, any of you regular folks out there suing over the shrinkage in your savings/investments? Maybe we should get in line like some of the Wall Street protestors and like, not pay our mortgages. After all, who really wants to pay money back?

How long before I can open my Bar?

More government regulations, more lawsuits and litigation will be the order of the day for awhile. Unless the new governmental employees after the other day really decide to reduce ridiculous intrusions on small businesses, you will only see the lawyers make out. This can be very discouraging from a free market standpoint. How do you compete when other countries markets are not saddled with the same burdens?

News Flash....Back to the Same Ol' Stuff

I just couldn't resist this and since it's one of those things that hit the news quickly and moves on (especially for those who are in it) thought I would jot it down before I forget. Apparently, GM (that's General Motors, at least for now) is jet setting around Europe and Asia or wherever they have to in an attempt to generate interest in a stock offering. It's interesting to note the jetting around is with private jets paid for with "GM's money". Really? After obtaining 45 billion dollars in future tax breaks to offset future profits, bragging about making money these days, what do they do? Go right back to the same old ways pissing money away.

Don't get me wrong. I think they are probably making better vehicle these days. I suppose they would have to go far enough away to convince others (since it won't be USA owned at that juncture) to purchase an interest. No sane person here would jump in. Even if the make money, they will end up being foreign owned and go the way other American icons (Budweiser) will go. More arrogance and government hypocrisy. When the government slams GM for spending money on their own, it's a problem, but when they use taxpayer money it's ok to joy rider around planet Earth. What a con. Oh, and by the way, when GM is bought out by whatever foreign interests get involved, that big building in Detroit get scuttled and moves to wherever the new foreign world headquarters will be and with that, move control over where GM cars will be built, i.e. not…here.

Break Up California!!!

Let's face it, they don't know how to or do not want to do anything about their present financial situation. They live in a different world, so we should have a contest to see who comes up with the best solution to the situation. There would be no more tax payer monies to go in that direction without real hard working folks watching the flow. The winner could, say, become king of their land. Maybe see if some other country would claim them. Mexico always thought it was theirs, no? How about breaking it up into several pieces the adjoining states could encompass? Of course, some of those areas may have their own problems and probably wouldn't want them.

Ooooo...oooooo! Call on me teacher, I know, I know....we could, like, maybe, pretend they're not there, like ignoring monsters in a fairy tale. After all, they spend money that's not there, or theirs, like there's no tomorrow, because let's face it, tomorrow is very far away......in a land far away, never, never land.....paying the piper tomorrow never comes out there.....

A Nice Day but Still Reading about Fallout

Driving home from some errands; got the windows down listening to Gene Ammons on the iPod playing "Canadian Sunset". A good old tune played by many artists. I like the other few versions I've heard. Another guy who didn't live long (cancer), got in trouble with the law on occasion (drugs) but taken for its moment, a good sound.

I get home to read some articles, one in particular I find of interest. Anyone ever heard of an economist named Melchior Palyi? Apologies to those who have, but I'll go with "I didn't think so". Neither did I until I read the article.

This gentleman predicted the financial crisis. How many times have we heard these storied after the fact...but in 1938. He indicated the problems started when the ratings agencies we know of today took over the credit ratings from the bankers. What would be the purpose of the agencies advocating good bond ratings to many that eventually went bust? You know the answer. Who supported the agencies? Too much power in centralizing government and my favorite, everyone should be in a home. Just try and tell that to folks who cannot get mobile enough today to move and get a job somewhere else.

There are other things, still harping on too much government regulations, everything from gas mileage requirements to silly warning stickers on everything. I suppose some businesses do get the breaks when they pony up with government but maybe with the changes in the congress there will be more gains towards the small business owner. We'll see.

Need to get by "judicial audacities" as well. There are too many judges imposing their own beliefs on rulings rather than on law.

I took another reading break, just came back. I read so much more than in my younger days. I fear I shall not be able to retain as much as I would like, especially when it comes to history. We weren't taught much about things that really occurred and these items, as I read them, seem unreal at times. Remembering them, if not for conversational purposes but just to satisfy one's intellectual content, may be difficult. When you're younger, you may have had the ability to retain more, but not necessarily the desire. Now that it appears more desirous, the ability….well, we can keep trying.

Who's Afraid of a Little Oyster?

So I am having lunch with the Colonel last week at one of our favorite oyster bars. You may remember I mentioned him as my neighbor in Diary/Dumbfoundedness. Anyway, there's nothing like a bucket of oysters and beer to start the day. Actually, it was already in the afternoon.

With all this talk of the problems in the Gulf, I figure two things. They wouldn't be serving these to you if they thought it was a problem, and we throw a little caution to the wind anyway. These babies (and I mean that literally, for some oysters are pulled a little early, given the timeframe) come from Apalachicola bay area anyway, far from the Gulf situation, which I hear may be alright anyway. If you like oysters, the Louisiana ones are (or were) my favorite. The proprietor of this establishment informs us the demand for the product has declined by a fairly decent amount over the last several months, but as things get back to whatever norm there is in this business, he expects it to pick up. God I hope so, making plans for another Florida Keys run in the not-too-distant future, so it would help.

The Colonial is my walking history book, and we have some interesting conversations about the past. It's the simple things that let you know life doesn't get any better.

I Thought a Luge was a Sled

Remember when cars had names like Mustang, Barracuda, Corvette, and Viper? Cars were a little simpler in days gone by, and they ran pretty good. Then we get to tinkering, think our excrement doesn't stink, and now, we worry about car emissions that couldn't hold a candle in carbon dioxide output to a week's worth of coal burning in Poland or China. I wasn't much of a car enthusiast in my younger days, but it would be nice to see cars that didn't have names that sound, well…..weak.

Don't Let the Door Hit You in the Rear!!

Ok, ok, I got it; with all this talk about a lame duck congress in session until January, we need to change the rule. As soon as you're elected you move in; as soon as you've lost…..get out!!

Lets face it, it's going to be tough enough to believe things will change all that much. Just listen to what's been going on in a week since the election, between the "koom-bay-yaing, let's work together stuff" to earmarking battles. At least we ought to get the lame ducks out of the way, because let's face it, they…don't ….care. Any damage they cause will not affect their health care coverage or their pensions, so send'em packing…now.

Can't Wait to Pay $15.00 for that Loaf of Bread

Yes, it is difficult to understand what the Federal Reserve is doing these days. We are dolts, sheep going to slaughter when it comes to understanding. I read something about the Fed almost daily, and it is written so as not to "unconfuse" me. You want to believe buying back bonds will do the country good against the likes of China, maybe. We'll just have to wait because since they supposedly operate on their own, we don't have much choice. Of course, don't be too afraid when you walk into Publix or wherever you shop next year. It may be frightening.

I may not be advocating walking in with gold bars, but you will need a whole lot more paper. China doesn't want to devaluate because nobody tells them what to do. So we devaluate at a time when more jobs go bye-bye. That'll show'em. Maybe now we can get some cheap products made around here to send overseas.

Is Anyone Driving that Car in Front of Me?

I am out and about visiting old acquaintances. It does not seem like things are improving in the construction sections much yet. I feel for them. While driving, I get behind someone whose head I cannot see, drifting between the lanes; pretty spooky. I swear, I didn't think anyone was driving the car. Once she (it was what appeared to be an older woman once I was able to pass her) decided to get in front of me again, of course she decides to drive slower than me. I tell you folks, these days nobody's driving much slower than me. It's always when you would like to be relatively on time to your next stop, not when you have no particular place to be at a certain time. I suppose much like life, you can only get to your destination as fast as the slowest car in front of you.

Anyway, I am late for the cutting of a few hairs. My usual guy isn't too concerned. It's a real "man's man" type place, although one of the guys wives now does women's hair. Karen thought she would try them and so far, so good. Anyway, a lot of "old salts" go in there. Nothing fancy, just down to earth manly stuff, FOX news on the TV, heads of stuffed animals around (my guy's also a taxidermist). I also make the quip about never wanting to fall asleep while he's cutting your hair…you may end up on the wall. Any of you guys still find a place like this, or are you ok with the commercial stuff? I never have to go in there and smell things, like in mainstream shops. That stuff makes me sneeze. You ask K, and she'll tell you the few times I walk through a mall with her, I walk around the perfume section, not through it. I'm not too allergic to things, but those places….

Anyway the tunes are a pumpin' good today. I like mostly everything I download, but once in a while, something comes on and I wonder what in hell made me record that one. Sometimes I play a head game by trying to remember the artist and the title of songs. I am disappointed when I cannot remember certain styles, especially since I used to retain it better. Sometimes the song comes back to me. Go figure.

When the barber asked me about the state of things, I tell him "see these new one story store front type buildings recently put up all around you?" He nods in the affirmative, and then I simply say "when they get rented out, you'll know things are getting better"

Life is a Left Turn, and Sometimes You Ain't Getting the Turn Signal

So, anyone catch a recent Johnny Carson skit about a politician giving a press release speech in answer to questions from the media. It's a You Tube slot, so it may be around for awhile. It's too bad we cannot do this, but it's a riot…and it's almost 30 years ago! In my estimation, Johnny's still the best, hands down. I would bet if he could be on stage as a deceased person, he would get higher ratings than anyone.

Yeah, it's just like they say; the politicians aren't going to let you in the lane to get a fair shot at what's going on, because they keep seeking the brass ring as a self serving position. They live in a different world with things like plausible deniability and misspoke words and don't even see the error of their ways.

The message of "be what you are and the message will convey itself" is either lost on them or so true no one can do much to avoid their misgivings save vote them out.

I'm Running Red Lights if this Keeps Up

So I get to a light and lo' and behold, another POS (that's piece of shit, for those who don't remember) pulls up along side and the noise emulating from this vehicle is well, starling. I heard it coming several hundred feet back and prayed the light would change, but no. I suppose law enforcement has better things to do, but they're really outta' be a law.

Look, I don't care what you listen to, but geez, does my sister in New Jersey have to hear it? The way that car was booming along, you would think a lot of parts would have shook out from under it.

The Lawn Police

I get down to my usually quiet dead end street and someone on the other side of the road it watering their lawn…on a Thursday…should only be doing on a Sunday this time of year. I am not the one to preach anything about breakin' the law, but again, it's not that all hell fired important to water the lawns that much this time of year. It wasn't a new one, and I suppose the timer wasn't adjusted. Besides, most of us are too damn old, semi or fully retired to give too much of a crap about how perfect the lawns should look. Lawns are for young people so their kids can run in the crunchy grass (that's St. Augustine grass for you non-Floridians). I do what I can with mine but a lot of it is under shade, and so I don't want to get too crazy over it (Astroturf anyone?)

Lugnutt and the Lawyers

Now, some of you who know me also know I am not a big fan in this arena. It's not that all lawyers are bad, but people all seem to cry foul when they see what lawyers are doing to them…until one represents them.

There are some many signs around town (usually in the more economically disadvantaged areas) about what these folks can do for you. No matter if it's your fault or otherwise, if it stinks enough, they'll trudge through the sludge to see what comes out on the other end.

It's no wonder we graduate more folks in law than we do engineers. And what products created by this situation are we trying to export? Maybe, as I read once years back in WSJ article, we could export lawyers, but I believe we would be disappointed over how many countries would not want them, or at least over what we would receive in return.

The Constitution, Jazz and Baseball

A good analogy to everything American, I hear these traits mentioned coincidently two times in a day, once in a Wynton Marsalis interview in a jazz book I am researching, and in a Ken Burns series called "Baseball". I am familiar with all three topics, and with respect to all, you would have to read or see how they transcend themselves into the fabric of our history and society, if you have not done so already.

The process of differences between the races began in the territories occupied by the French and English and after the not so "Civil War". Classes of mix race people began to see the separation of what was now considered white and black. A real tragedy. We simply did not wish to recognize multi-layered societies of people, exactly what the Constitution, while not happening at first, was supposed to lay out…i.e., all men would (eventually) be created with inalienable rights. The woman would get on their horse later towards equality.

You Can Take the Boy out of the Bronx, but…

For me, the situation is our environment. Not that I can complain, for you see I thought everyone grew up like I did. Concrete all around you, the multi-layered society entrenched around us all. We just didn't know any different. Going to visit an aunt (the only one who didn't live in the concrete jungle) barely into upstate New York; you may as well have gone half way around the world.

Getting back to the homestead, what did a bunch of 6-12 year olds know but baseball, and the seasons of sports? This race thing would have to wait until later. After all, we're just kids trying to have fun; the hate could start later, when we would all know better.

We seem to have spent a good portion of our history condemning, enslaving, penalizing a whole race (or races) of folks, and then, after rationally realizing the err of our ways, we let whole groups of them take advantage of a system that has done less harm to those very same folks. I have tried my whole life to take'em as they come, and that seems to have served me well for the most part. Nothing is 100 per cent. Environment can be a major factor, or misleading, but simply speaking; two wrongs don't make a right.

A Non-Polemic Approach

In a discussion with some of our offspring the other day, the subject of taxes was broached. I listened for awhile, not saying a word, and finally, I got my "in", so to speak. "Well, no one wants to pay taxes", one said. I was reminded of an article I had read not too long about this very subject, which indicated this argument was not true. In fact, it would depend on who was having the discussion, for surely, as was mentioned, if you want public services you need some form of taxation with representation.

I believe the discussion could go on forever, for the ability to continuously and exactly determine the "bell curve" of fairness based on one's status, income, political motivation always seem to justify the means of such discussions. I merely suggest any argument can be right or wrong, and ethically and/or intellectually unfinished, if I may quote from another source. As I have also mentioned several times, the skin has in a particular situation also affects one's attitude on a particular matter.

When People Agree with Me, I Feel I Must be Wrong

To quote an Oscar Wilde "ism", I read a blog comment from another offspring of ours about part of my first "Diary" book. It seems the term Tea Party's been thrown around much these days. It's too bad it took so long for so many of us to decide to "get involved" to some degree in the way Congress decides to run our lives. After all, the Tea Party did not create the problems. For my own part, it's a timing thing (coincidence?). When you have the time, you make the time to talk it up more, or babble on like these words do. At least you take less time to play video games.

I put it to you it's not so much a tea party attitude as much as how you want to live your lives. If it is that we prefer less government, less rules and regulations which will hamper growth and having more control over how the monies are spent, then serve me some China Black tea and keep it coming.

Then again, if you agree with the above too much, then we have to have more discussion on the alternatives, because whatever your fearless leaders can give, they can take away. So no, the idea of calling some people tea partiers is only a statement used to describe the way many felt all along. Maybe we just say, how about the "We're Tired of you Congress Folks Yapping with Your Piehole party, so listen up to us folks"?

Ok, this is starting to sound like some of the first time around, so I'll stop for awhile.

Why Stencil "Compact" on the Concrete Parking Stops?

While I am listening to "Foghat" on the pod, I search for a parking space. I never pay attention to the word "compact", which is marked on the concrete And, judging by the size of the vehicles occupying those spaces neither does everyone else. I park next to a Ford Expedition with a young woman getting out of the car with kids. The back window of the car is loaded with stickers, all of which are pet peeves of mine. First, the "my child is an honor student at some school…who do they think they are trying to impress? The kids aren't reading it, and if they think anyone in traffic behind you cares…Mozart must be rolling over in his grave. Next, we have the soccer balls with the kids name/number in them. Then we have the stick figures of everyone in the family, including the dogs and cats. Next, in the "Ya' Gotta" Be Shittin' Me" department, an "NSB" sticker. In Florida folks, that stands for New Smyrna Beach, a place I took the kids a hundred years ago when it was a better place to go. What an armpit, but I ain't saying where I hang out now, because I want folks with this kind of crap on their cars to keep going to NSB!!

Panic before the Panic

I don't mind listening to the media pundits going through their exercises about all sorts of topics. I used to think the term "publish or perish" was reserved for academia, but I believe everyone who has a show writes them, as well as most of their guests.

On the surface, it doesn't seem like a problem, except everyone's in competition for your time (and your wallets-hey, listen to me, go buy this book so you can read this). Lately, there's been a lot of talk about dooms day scenarios where in the not too distant future, economists in some camps are predicting outrageous claims of a sort of hyperinflation. Can you imagine that? I know we have to have a little understanding of these things, but come on folks, if the type of inflation comes in this form; the only thing the local supermarket will take from you is gold for payment.

I suppose it is only human nature to prepare when it may seem too late, the talk can be spooky, and the panic can lead to a sort of freezing effect on your normally rational thought process. Some folks say gold will go to $10,000 an ounce. When I cannot say for certain, but you better go buy a whole bunch.

Look, I am a "through out the highs and lows" kind of' guy, so while I am not going to tell you it's going to be a picnic, ask yourself what good is it going to do a lot of companies if they price their products where no one can afford them? You won't be able to pay $100 for a loaf of bread, because the bread company couldn't afford to pay their workers enough money for them to buy the bread. We'll see.

So What Are Exchange Traded Funds?

All the rage on the tube about ETF's, you'd think it was a second coming or something. In reading about them, trading on whole stock indexes at various exchanges may sound exciting, but do you know enough about them? I see ads where they say you shouldn't settle for 15 or 20 exchange choices, you need a hundred of'em!! Wow wee, just what I need; more confusion about a product I am suspecting a lot of professionals haven't yet become proficient. You see all these youngin's on the screen sitting around the park of a big office type building with their lap tops (like they wouldn't trade at their desk?) pushing the buttons buying, selling and trading away, like it's no big deal. I don't know; call me old fashioned, but if the brokerages aren't making' out like bandits on this one…and we know they have to, because the bonus checks, well, they gotta' keep coming in; mama needs a new pair of shoes, or a Mercedes or something,

Hey, I'm not saying don't make a living, and god knows you have to do something to save a couple of bucks. Just be careful of too many choices. After awhile, you go full circle and they start to sound familiar. Don't forget the old adage, "buy low, sell high!!" Good fortune hunting.

The Constitution

There are folks out there thinking, "Maybe this document's a little dated and we need something else for the times". From my vantage point, I would not support that argument. We have been back on the citizenship of our President of late, and while I have heard and seen a few sides of this issue, there are too many questions resolving the matter, which can lead to more questions. Some will say we don't need to address this issue, in light of the other problems we are facing. I wish it were that easy and we could put it to bed. By the time this makes print, something else will take its place. There are many lawsuits out there, and would not know how this will end, but it is taking a lot of effort on parties to distort, hide or fabricate facts. How many of us really believe everything on the Internet? You didn't believe newspaper media for a long time, and look where the printed word is heading.

What I do believe is the subject needs closure, so the Fourteenth Amendment as well as the other 26 Amendments (including one repeal) hold and bind our country. It is not a perfect system, but it is ours, and as I may have mentioned before, it's what got us to the dance. We may find ourselves in a different light in the world today, with economies of rising nations trying to place their mark in the world. I can't say I blame them. It is a good thing to have trade, and know while we may be the main engine driving output, others are catching up. It's hard to stay on top of the heap forever without some company. While I may not agree with much about this administration, it is a hard job and we can at least attempt to respect the man and the underlying responsibility of the position.

Read, Gather an Opinion, Stick to It...maybe

So I read an article about the guesswork of our so-called experts in the political science area. Lo' and behold, the word "guesswork" I use above is correct, for many of these experts were wrong in their predictions about their choices. There were a lot of choices and lot of misses.

The next part I could almost predict. There was an abundance of overconfidence, "disproportionately analyzing the evidence" (what the hell) and just plain wrong. I always suspect when you're lucky, you try to come off as a bit good and vice versa, and this is ok, at least if you can keep your ego in check and are honest with yourself. Facts which may have been relevant in their analysis were ignored (the ego again, or non-sharing of opinion). It said they become prisoners of their own convictions. I suppose we all have this happen from time to time, but we aren't paid huge sums of money as these folks are, to be so wrong. As the article goes to state, you might as well flip a coin. So feel free to read a little about things which may be of interest, give and opinion in discussion, and don't worry too much about being wrong. Life will go on, and the odds of you being in the right are as good as anyone's.

You want to dip into that GM stock again?

More problems on the pension front, especially in states like California and New Jersey. The folks who wrote those laws knew what pot of gold was waiting for them at the end of the rainbow. Still, we send jobs away because under the guise of costs, it costs less to produce in a far away land, but let's face it, CEO's pay is alarming, and so what's the real deal? While line jobs go begging because we worry about tax and health and regulatory consequences, the top of the food chain takes an even bigger chunk away.

Hell, look at this GM thing we've got going now. A company that thought the good times would never end to the point of being stubborn found itself in bankruptcy, succumbing to such tactics as to keep what, too many jobs from going away, or helping the unions keep what shrinking presence they represent. Now they are profitable, all at tax payer expense. Tell me, the regular folks who lose out after bankruptcy, the prepackaged arrangement firms with their attorneys make, the too big to fail fiasco!! How much more of this can we stand? Now they want to go public again. The main reason for GM' pre-bankruptcy situation is, like most other companies, no sales and no money to borrow. The entire present situation was done to keep unions happy. I assume those of you who lost the first time couldn't think it could ever happen again. In the event of a future electric car and/or economic bust, you will lose your money first.

This electric car thing seems hastily put together to compete with foreign models, which seem more efficient and cheaper. Buy why worry about cost when you don't have to answer to anyone about how much it is to produce. I suppose the "beautiful people will have to seen driving on of these disasters around (probably get paid to do it). Oh, and don't forget how much it will save the earth. Not in this or many, many lifetimes. The temperature gauge of earth won't move a tenth of a degree if we all goose-stepped in line to buy one of these, so if you want one, do it for yourself, not because it's the "in-thing" to do.

In case you haven't heard, there's a "new" oil field discovery in Iraq. Interesting, isn't it? We go over there and kill our selves in lives and massive amounts of money, only to know now a whole new city opens to this discovery in the southern portion of Iraq. You know those BP guys are right in the mix on this one, along with the Chinese, the Turks and I am certain we need to be in there as well. We go do the dirty work in a country everybody condemns us for undertaking, yet how many Chinese soldiers were defending Iraq? They were too busy helping Iran. No, my friends, oil is not going to be replaced as the major source for some time to come.

Some Things are Always in Vogue

The budget should be balanced, the Treasury should be refilled, public debt should be reduced, the arrogance of officialdom should be tempered and controlled, and the assistance to foreign lands should be curtailed lest Rome become bankrupt.

People must again work instead of living on public assistance."

--- Cicero, 55 BC

Does anyone know how many times this has been passed around the Internet or various sources? It's nice, and worthwhile, but it needed to be hammered home before the debacle. In a more homogeneous atmosphere with a few thousand folks may make it seem easier to accomplish, but still we must try.

Technology Kills

Just ask the Post Office. I can't believe what I hear about their numbers. Look, it's not like they didn't know this was coming. Just ignore it (the Internet) and it will go away? Cry to your parents (government) and make them play fair? What a joke. Take it private. End of story.

We are all faced with the inevitable end to our livelihoods these days (unless you receive a pension in places like New Jersey and

California or a CEO of a major corporation), so how do we prepare for it? It is not easy. I "saw a light" or had a "wison" many years back. I really don't remember how or why (no offense to Mom and Dad, but like most folks of the era, there was little they could do financially other than "get us to the dance", no small feat with four of us as it was). But I was able to take care of business while always wondering when it would end. (A fatalistic approach?). I may not have always thought it would be technology (competition, which can come in technological form) but at least we can still take care of business, i.e.; the roof over my/K's head. For how much longer, who knows? What with health care issues (we seem fairly healthy at this writing) her side business trying to gear up and lingering back items, I don't know. I have always managed to go it alone (with K) and don't know how our situation would differ if things changed for the worse. I believe with a little encouragement, a positive attitude and (gulp!) a little luck, things will work out the way they should. As I may have mentioned before, tomorrow is promised to no one, and you are in the space you're supposed to occupy. Play them cards as they are dealt!!

Don't Give Up the Dream

I just read a blog from one our offspring's websites. In it, it talks about a potential review of the first "Diary" along with thoughts about where he and his family are at this juncture in their lives. There was also another comment from one of his fellow graduate students, similar in content pertaining to the world that may be some day. The questions, answers, where your place is in the grand scheme of things are covered. "The question to everyone's answer is usually asked from within", to borrow from the Steve Miller Band.

Sometimes, the more you learn, the more questions there are, and there is no such thing as a quick question, only potentially quick answers. In his case, the struggle to continue graduate studies seem to conflict with the daily routine of raising two daughters and his wife trying to balance work and a home life as well. I can feel for them. I remember a time…well, it was a time gone by, so I will stick to the present and future. They seem to go forward like many of us, with some doubts and potentially some fear of the unknown. To this, as I have said in the past, is "get up, dress up and show up", and things will right themselves.

The Soul of America

I like jazz. You may have inferred that from previous pages and in the first edition. I played a little in school, rock, some jazz, with a few bands, although honesty didn't believe it would amount to anything. There were nights I thought this would be a great way to go through life. Other nights, well, it sucked, but I never lost the love to listen.

Over the years, I have accumulated what I would consider a modest collection for such an amateur. I like the older versions of smaller "trap" bands or groups, not too much into the big band stuff, although I admire it all. It seems to fill the gaps the best when rock isn't the right feel of the moment. In reading biographies about some of those who have since departed…when you sum it up, it seems impossible to be born with the ability to play it without life's experiences getting a lot of the credit as a foundation. Yes, you can be born with a genius ability to play the notes, have perfect pitch and so forth, but without life's travels, your playing may expose you as a fraud. To those who struggle with this assessment and are in the arena, I mean this in the kindest way.

God Has No Religion

So I checked the obituaries this morning…I wasn't there…another day on planet Earth. I borrowed the obit comment from one or two older sources than me, mainly from my good friend Sam. He lives in North Florida, and we have on occasion got together to check out some of the more colorful watering holes on this peninsula (he has been in quite a few more than me… sorry bud, nothing wrong with that, but it's the truth.

I think when Mahatma Gandhi made the chaptered statement above, he was thinking of guys like Sam (and maybe me at times). Sam and I go back a good 30 or so, and prior to our meeting, God took it upon himself to send him (on more than one occasion) to a part of the world in the sixties that, shall we say, wasn't a tourist attraction. After going through these things, well, every day's a good day eventually, because you know you're in the bonus round of life. Anyway, we worked together for many years, and still correspond. We like the Florida Keys and make every attempt to be there whenever possible. A good friend and confidant, I hope I do not have to toast a fallen comrade for many, many years to come (nor he to me). Maybe Kat (his wife) and Karen can help keep us in line. Well see. Sometimes it seems like it has been a long road, but as I mentioned above, no obit notices yet.

I cannot speak for anyone else, and I know this chapter about religion is not what Gandhi had in mind when he said it, but I am probably as close to being agnostic as anything. There is something out there, a feeling of "things happen for a reason" as K likes to remind from time to time. Religion and disease have had more influence on death and destruction in the world than anything, and in the "fight for right" and to "find the cure", it all becomes a matter of semantics…they're all dead anyway. Even in one of Mr. Dorsey's latest books, his main character Serge says to "cherish freedom of religion…protect it from religion". How deep is that, eh?

If we truly wanted to stop the violence, we could, but then, where would the "Lords of War" be? I challenge anyone to tell us we are truly trying to stop these things. I don't think human nature will allow it to happen; again, not knowing for certain after our time is over.

How much do You Really Want to Know?

You ever see those search engines that talk about finding out who might be looking for you? Maybe that's more than you want to know. An old lover? An estate of a deceased rich uncle? More like a creditor or lawyer looking to slap some injunction on you.

So while I am writing this afternoon, Sam calls me to say something about the first "Diary". I don't know if I want to hear it, but he says he hasn't read enough yet (just finished one book and starting on mine, says he's not as talented as me, who can juggle 2-3 books at once). He thought there was a proofing error in the book (a sentence that says "in" instead of "is") and it could be, but then again, I can do those things on purpose as well. I let him know it didn't matter much to me; we've all seen greater works with errors. We may feel "grammatically challenged" at times, so a little error now and then keeps you in check. Anyway, I will have to wait for more of what I may not want to know (with respect to Mr. Wilde's quotation earlier) later on.

Sam was curious if I was at a book signing. I said sure thing. Can't you hear the noise in the background? I am at a Borders Book Store with a table in front. There's a sign over my head that says "Tim Dorsey will be here at 4PM, so please stop by and sign in, and you may as well buy and sign my book while you wait"…what….not funny?...K thought it was…maybe you have no sense of humor. I think more moments have to be humorous in the remaining chapters, and will endeavor to be so.

Ok, so I Lied, this Chapter may not be Funny

Maybe it will be funny; I think I shall leave it up to you. There are some media pundits out there who are really taking it to the tea baggers and such. Do they really have to go down this line for ratings? They are saying some mean things about most of you common sense folks and either you don't care because it's nothing more than hot air, or you like watching the circus on TV (as in "clowns").

They sound like they're in kindergarten slamming and smacking folks down because they don't seem to have much else to say (you're a doody head; no you are!!- You remember this stuff?). They truly live in their own world, and if you didn't laugh at them, you might feel a bit sorry instead, but remember, someone is paying them, probably a whole lot more dough than most of us see, to be this way.

I Hate it when this Happens

So I hear on the news today about no more lame duck congress periods. Didn't I mention this above? Remember…you heard it first here. Well no, actually it came up in 1933 after congress passed the 20th Amendment, shortening the time congress could use the lame duck session. There were some disastrous periods it was used, as in the period between the James Buchanan and Abraham Lincoln presidencies, which sped up the beginning of the not so Civil War. Anyway, it wasn't my goal to dwell on this here, just merely point out my previous mention of the idea. Until yesterday, I hadn't heard anyone mention it. Maybe I just don't hang with the right people.

What happened to Grace and Class?

Many of you have probably noticed of late the length to which some of our leaders, sports figures and even some of our media personalities will go in order to stay in the spotlight. It's tragic. It sends a terrible message to those who also think they are "greater than the game". Some of these "hangers-on" are resorting to some amazing tactics and other than the obvious reasons (at the feast of egos, everyone still leaves hungry); they need to get a grip.

The Man in the Glass

Author Unknown

When you get what you
want in your struggles for
self

And the world makes you
king for a day,

Just go to a mirror and
look at yourself

And see what THAT man
has to say.

For it isn't your father or
mother or wife

Whose judgment upon

you must pass,

The fellow whose verdict
counts most in your life

Is the one staring back
from the glass.

Some people might think
you're a straight-shooting
chum

And call you a wonderful
guy.

But the man in the glass
says you're only a bum

If you can't look him
straight in the eye.

He's the fellow to please,
never mind all the rest

For he's with you clear up
to the end

And you've passed your
most dangerous, difficult
test

If the man in the glass is
your friend.

You may fool the whole
world down the pathway
of years and life

And get pats on the back
as you pass

But your final reward will
be heartache and tears

If you've cheated the man
in the glass.

Unknown Author

For politicians, the spoiled brats of sports and
well, just about for the lot of us. The above
poem needs to be placed where you can see it
every day rise to greet a new one. I may beg to
differ on the unknown author; my original copy
of this (with some slight revisions above due to
the author) was written by Mr. Dale Wimbrow.

I merely make reference to Mr. Wimbrow
because of the credit he deserves in this, and
the fact that a park in Roseland, Florida was
named after him. He also wrote a couple of
books and several songs. He died in 1954.

So, Where are you gonna' Live?

I see where St. Louis has replaced Camden, NJ as the nation's most dangerous city to live in the US. I wonder how Karen's sister (lives in the St. Louis area) cares about these things. I don't usually get too excited about them. Florida has its share of "high on the bum list" items, and in reality, if you're in the wrong place at the wrong time, well, you know. It seems the data is collected by the FBI and computes its output based on the most violent crimes. Of course, some criminologists will dispute these things. Usually the ones who live in the area I suppose, every time statistics bring out the best or worse in a city, town, harem or wherever, you get the "data is skewed" argument or in the case of the "best" in a category, "yes, we love it here and we want you to stay away so you don't mess up the stats".

Buy hey, what's in a city? It's a place you live, maybe work; maybe you like it no matter what the statisticians' charts and graphs show. You know, many of us feel like we are losing our stature in the world anyway, so what's the difference? Twenty years ago, it was Japan, and now, in spite of some great accomplishments, China overtakes their GDP to number two in the world. In an article I read over the weekend, China, in some ways, has already overtaken us in some categories, and "they" say it won't be long before the rest of important slots are also owned by them. Just look at domestic product growth. Hell, even the commies don't have to fudge too much there. We'll have to wait and see.

I say, it's ok. Look at the facts. The Western Hemisphere nations, in general, have been on top for a few hundred years of late. Now, who does China, India and the like want to emulate? Not that we should be going down without a competitive fight, mind you, but we have set the standard for others to follow. Nothing in the history of the world has ever been accomplished, albeit not always good, like this nation has done. I hope we can learn to accept the new boundaries that are being drawn for everyone in the new world, because it is changing. I don't want to sound so harsh as to simply say "adapt or die", but there are issues which need to be addressed now; not next month or next year, so that we at least maintain a major presence in most areas of world wide thinking and processing.

Ok, ok; I'm getting off the soap box for now.

War

This is a pet peeve of mine of which I may be in the minority. I shall take my chances. I play a few computer games. The doctors will tell you it's good for motor skills or some other brain exercising (not to mention carpel tunnel) so I will accept the reasoning. Of course, the kind of games I play a five year old could beat my keister big time.

Anyway, my point is, the games I choose to play do not depict combat soldiers killing and maiming each other. I will pause now for the oooo's and ahhh's from the gaming industry folks who would give a rat's ass about this feeling over making millions. My feeling is, if you want to shoot at aliens, spaceships and monsters (still not officially in earth's picture, so ok) then ok. But these kids (and young adults), they don't have a right (with respect to those who play who have been in those real life scenarios).

The same mommies and daddies who wouldn't think of sending their kids off to do the dirty work don't mind if their kids keep pushing the reset button on war just to keep them out of their way? Oh, I know, these games are not for "teeny-weenie ones" (the way a law professor once called those under the age of 18…no I am not an attorney, just thought I would arm myself will some of their thinking processes). Now who's kidding whom?

As "The Kid from Brooklyn" says, "think about it!!!"...

Redundancy

As the white cell count is finally winning the battle (slight cold) I decide to give the treadmill another go at running to nowhere.
It's an old story. As the Mike and Mike boys on the sports tube blab on about the hurt feelings and arguments these so-called "professionals" get into, I have to change the station. I mean really, I turn this station on so I get at least somewhat of a decent cardiovascular workout (subject to occasional leg and back cramps) in some bizarre attempt to also keep the heart pumping. When these types of discussions invade, I weep for the youth of America. I don't know what can be done about it, but at least I can watch something like the news, which makes no sense, since the news is why I switched to sports in the first place! Of course, if all else fails, the boom box sits right below the TV on the shelf. That is what usually goes on about half the times anyway, since I can at least control those sounds.

Some of these sports figures just forgot what it was like before their lives changed financially. There are no better than many of these Hollywood types who give too much opinion and not enough good service. But I suppose in this day and age this is what we have come to expect. In the case of some of these players, it's "I can't play for this coach or with this player". Oh really? Where does it say in your contract you won't be paid if you are on a team you feel have personnel of which you can't get along? Maybe it's time to stick little clauses like this in these documents. I believe as a professional in any endeavor, part of the process involves adapting to your situation, especially one where you have little or no control.

I believe it's time to hit the showers.

Even rats leave a sinking Ship

So I see today more of the administration's economic team is departing. It's interesting, because they come in, do their (dirty?) work, get praises from the folks who still remain (for how long?) and they're gone. I don't understand; if they did such a grand job at designing laws and bills (many don't want), why are they leaving? Why do they always get a pat on the back from those who are the only ones who seem to think it was a job well done (until the "patters" are out, then the book writing begins). I know; they have to spend more time with their families, or they knew they'd be coming in only for short period of time to do whatever good/damage they could, then leave. After all, who's going to remember them? Back to academia, where tenure reigns, and you get to write books that will sell less than this one (hopefully).

Let's face it; it's a very exclusive club, and you and I are not members.

The Problem is on your end, Sir

Oh God!!...We can't watch the Soprano's tonight!
        Or, what happens when the cable
        Decides to take a hike!!!

It was Sunday morning, and the folks, who hadn't visited in several years (we always seemed to go to them) were heading back to New Jersey (yes, some people still actually CHOOSE to live there). On the way back from the airport, we stopped at the grocery store for some things and headed home.

Lo and behold… all the modern conveniences of our 21st century lifestyles were blinking away (except for the ones that drain us with seemingly constant battery requirements)…. The power had gone off and come back on. Who knows how long it had been out, but no matter, for it only takes a few moments and then after you check everything you can fix, you find out the computer and TV cable lines are not working. You do all the usual things your computer expert friend or "cable guy" tells you on the computer by pulling out wires and counting out sixty seconds while you are in the usual uncomfortable position under the computer tables (I swear, that's the longest sixty seconds of one's life).

When the usual things don't work, you call your speedy cable company back. They tell you those words you never want to hear… "It's only your line sir, because we have received no other calls"…or "it must be the cable company's problem, because the

computer lines are not reporting any problems"....
Now I ask myself how it always seem to be only our
lines. Ok, I say to myself, it's no big deal. I didn't really
<u>need</u> to watch that old black and white movie I
planned to see today.

Now you are faced with a big dilemma; Remember all
those times you told yourself you would get some of
that reading done when the time was right, and now
you find yourself begging for an excuse to say it's <u>still</u>
not the right time. Ah...I know...H-O-N-E-Y-D-U-E-
S!!...Those things you told your significant other you
promised to do yesterday, and by golly, you did them,
but now!!...He/She's gotcha' again!

By now, you are praying for the computer and cable
gods to miraculously work their magic by simply
working all by themselves, because that event has
happened before, if not very frequently. You begin to
think "hell if I was George Bush or someone like that,
ain't no way I would be <u>suffering</u> like this even on a
Sunday...and oh, yes, just TRY to deduct the day's
loss of cable time from the bill when you go to pay it...

Go work out, stay out of your significant other's way,
and hope like hell you have an understanding wife (as
in my case). Pray they allow you time to do things like
write this nonsense just to enjoy these quiet moments
or read <u>all</u> the paper today (since you normally only
look at the sports section or how crummy your stocks
are doing). Hope she (my case again) brings home
some work to do from the job that she would normally
not do and doesn't pay too much attention at trying to
grab extra time out of your hide! Hope some buddy
calls because maybe, just maybe somewhere off in a

distant galaxy, or just down the street, someone else actually has the same problem with the cable gods and is looking to escape with you.

STARDUST

I wake up about 4 AM thinking of oldies which so many folks love to listen to, and how many are used in commercials these days. I am not even a fan of a lot of these tunes, but you can't help but appreciate the sounds. If you youngins' think those advertisers made up some of those songs, well, you ain't been around too long. You don't hear too many songs nobody recognizes, so why it that? Just a thought, especially at 4 AM.

Extremes

So K's looking at the news when I walk in the room. She wants to see if there's a big fuss at the airport about the opt-out day for the pat downs vs. the TSA folks (I have avoided this subject because I plan on a plane ride with her next week so I can make my own evaluations, although the more frequent flyers may have a differing opinion).

I don't know if there will be much more than the usual extreme issues regarding this or most any news matter. If you take out the highs and the lows of media broadcast, well, you would have no broadcast.

The norm is boring. Without extremes and everyone's desire for their fifteen minutes….no news.

Now, go read a book or watch a good old movie or maybe write a book, even if it's to you. More on the travel hiccups after the trip.

Everybody accuses, everybody denies

It gets pretty old doesn't it? Some football player gets accused of being a "dirty" player, the accused players coach says something like "we don't teach that in our coaching, we do not condone that type of play", or something to that effort. You can apply that to business, lawsuits, i.e. "he/she's a crook, and we categorically deny, blah, blah…" It gets old.

GRUMP-A

For the last couple of years, I have tried to make it a habit every rising morning to ask myself this question;

Am I in the obit pages today?...No, not that…

Do I wish to think positively or negatively today?

It is not an easy thing to do all the time, but I felt that it needs to be addressed on a daily basis, simply because positive thoughts always outweigh negative ones. Of course, this is all notwithstanding the names our grandchildren call us from time to time in their own version of the English language. I get varying degrees of sounds for the name, "grandpa". By this I mean words like "Elmo", and "grump a".

Now I know we all have our ways of dealing with crumb – crunchers. As a result of way we interact with the little darlings, we get branded with certain names and phrases like the ones I described above. They may not even mean or know what they say but nonetheless they say it anyway. How we interpret their meaning depends on who is doing the interpreting. I tend not to highlight and repeat the sounds these little ones call me, but K, oh no, she can't wait to reiterate everything they say with more resonance in the pronunciations blurted by them.

"Did you hear what she called you? … GRUMP-A!!" I tell you, I don't know how she hears those sounds. Maybe I just block them out. I think she just emphasizes the sounds to poke a little fun at my expense. It's okay though, it's real funny, and the kids seem to like it. I am sure a lot of you out there have had similar experiences. I don't think I'm so grumpy, but I suppose others will have to be the judge in these matters.

...And So it Goes...

I have just returned from a trip to the late nineteenth to the early twentieth century. The series on "Baseball" always puts me "in the zone", so to speak. I must admit, I knew very little about the nuances of it history, and now, coming full circle, I find myself in the same position.

But somewhere in between, it was marvelous. You knew all the players, their numbers, stats, etc. I even wrote something about my feelings on the matter a few years back. My thoughts:

The Fall of 2007

With all the talk of baseballs' present situation.....my thoughts.

For an aging boomer brought up in the Bronx, baseball was it. There were other "seasons" of things to do, but nothing triumphed the late spring through early fall like some manner of play. For the record, I am by no means an expert (although my wife thinks it's amusing I can recite the names of the a certain team's starting and sometimes not starting players of my youth by name and numbers on the uniform; heck, I tell her, all of us could back then, no big deal!).

I began to think back to a time, say the turn of the 20th century. What was considered baseball then consisted of few professional teams, only a handful of major league cities with parks, and by parks, I use the term loosely, as grounds keeping was not the skill it is today. You had to hit the ball a ton ("dead ball" era) with a not so special bat, and share gloves with players on both sides. Travel was nothing of comfort…you get the idea. Most pitchers pitched sometimes in consecutive days, even on the same day……again, no surprises to most baseball history buffs. In those days, the drug of choice was alcohol, by no means and enhancer to performance.

As baseball progressed in the early to middle part of the century, you had some improvements. It would have been interesting to see who would have ultimately made it to the "Hall" had organizations like the Negro League merged into the major leagues, but that's history. Up until my time and a little beyond, most players lived and socialized with the regular folk, even using public transportation. Since they weren't paid much more than the working folk at the time, they held down jobs during the off season.

I suppose my point is, change came when people wanted more as much as the players. We wanted to see records broken, so the ball got arguably livelier, the parks began to shrink so there were more home runs, the pitchers didn't have to pitch as much, and relief work becomes an art in various parts of the game. We want more cities with a franchise, and of course with this adds the desire for a winning team. For many years, the dreaded "reserve clause", tying a player to club for life and receiving pay only the owner desired, was the rule. It was to be this way in other industries as well, which eventually made it possible for unions to be created and prosper.

Enter the Curt Flood era, and players demands start the swing process in their favor, ultimately leading to free agency. Players now distance themselves from the ordinary folks because they have or want to, and can afford to do these things. We pay the inflated price to watch in many cases a deflated performance.

So along comes the next great thing to sooth the ego's of aging, average, and in some cases, great players to go out there and put up some amazing numbers (check the stats on some average players over short periods of time; pretty amazing stuff). The steroid thing becomes the spectacle of our times. Drugs have been such an integral part of our lives. It will make your kids achieve in school, and persuade everything on the tube's advertised list to cure what ails us, real or imagined. Don't forget ways to ease the pressure to figure how to make those sales goals for the company so the boss is happy so you can get that bonus.

We cannot go to a game without bringing our distractions along, i.e.; the cell phone or the kids playing a computer game, because the game is too much a chess match for the way we have become accustomed to thinking. Some of us may well ask again, "where have you gone, Joe DiMaggio, but even Mr. D. had his issues. Of course in those days, the press may have been more forgiving than today's Paparazzi style media.

The famous account of the Black Sox scandal found those men not guilty (records of testimony somehow "lost" from the files) since they actually broke no laws of their time according to a jury of their peers. Yet for right or wrong, Judge Landis, the final law of the baseball land and first commissioner at the time, decided to police baseball and bar these players. It is in this way that because we may never know the true extent of the present day allegations that baseball will regulate itself again. It becomes more fodder for a media designed to hype their opinions on us. Some players will suffer more than others and, depending on what city you live and what team one supports, opinions will vary as to the extent of the final decisions on each player involved. One can only hope location of the some of baseball icon's final resting place doesn't become the Hall of Shame.

With all due respect to the George Wills' and Bob Costas' of the world who will write with much more insight and in far more depth than the scope of this piece, I rest my case. It will take its place in history with subsequent events that will occur in this arena, and it is my fervent desire for it to survive.

Mohammed

So, K and I are driving to one of our children's home for Thanksgiving and I notice I don't have a lot of petrol. K says she hopes there is a gas station available because of the holiday. Although it's Thanksgiving I figure there ought to some stations open. I notice there are more than some stations open. I eventually stop and fill up. When I got back in the car, I thought about it and said to K "of course there are gas stations and convenience stores open on Thanksgiving. We have the most common name in the world to thank for this situation. What else would Mohammed do on a day like today? They don't celebrate these holidays, I suppose, and if they do, there's plenty of time later in the day. In the meantime, they are going to make money". Hell, it's what I'd been doing if I was working.

It was not an attempt at any disrespect, but after the way I explained it in the "what else are they gonna' do mode", she thought it was pretty hilarious. In addition, what's the hurry to get to grandma's house (if that's where you are heading) anyway? Grandma, if she's any kind of modern-day elder, is probably not baking your favorite pie or making turkey the way you remembered as a young one. She (and hopefully grandpa as well) are probably out having some fun themselves. I mean, your elders did all that holiday stuff for so many years so what do they have more to prove?

I wish this segment could've been captured a little more dramatically, as it was pretty funny listening to it on my recorder in the car. I use it from time to time so I can transfer these messages into words. I guess you had to be there.

Always and Never

These two words are to the point where they are almost superfluous. I mean, I understand when you say "always cover your mouth when you cough", or "never put that stick in your eye". Other than statements as obvious as these, the words are at best, statements of opinion, and not fact.

How many times have you heard, "we've always done it that way", or "I will never stop loving her". In truth, how can you know something can't be done a different way if you never tried and as far as love, well, never is a long, long time.
At the risk of sounding hypocritical, may all of us who are with whom we are with and are happy and stay that way. Maybe the "love" example was a push, but you get my drift. Maybe the words used in the way we describe our day-to-day dealings need some addressing. Sometimes "always" takes a more traditional approach which may be good for the soul, or the organization or community, and it, like love, may be a good thing.

If you can think of ways these words are used in your everyday lives and think there could be room for improvement as such, then that is all there is to say on the matter.

So, when are you going to know where they Stand?

I had seen some discussion about some folks who lost in the recent elections which make claims about too many early votes being counted when all the ideas and debates hadn't taken place. I believe if you vote your ticket, as many folks did or still do for many years, you may be guilty of these accusations since you may be missing out on some folk's views akin to your own in spite of their party affiliation.

In one of the Clinton elections, I was standing in line waiting for the doors to open and a conversation began between a young lady voting for the first time, an "old timer", and "middle aged timer", the latter being me. Mind you, some folks would not discuss their selections with strangers, simply for fear of being caught in one of those "how could you vote for that guy/gal discussions". You could be made to feel uninformed. However, this young lady was adamant about her choice of Mr. Clinton. The old timer and I were curious (we were not voting for Mr. C then, see, I admitted it) and I decided to venture out there and ask why. Her main reasoning was because she wanted to vote for the winner.

I had to let that sink in for a few moments because while I understand the mentality of the situation, no wonder politicians would rather certain segments from our classes should (or should not, depending on what you main voting base consists) be allowed to vote. This can be a powerful feeling (wanting to vote for the winner) to overcome if your choice is the upstart or the other guy/gal.

Fast forwarding to today about the early voting. Did some people not get all the information the needed to make an informed decision, or did they want to "vote for the winner", whether in a month or a week before the voting day deadline? Was the scenario presented by a candidate with sour grapes?

I believe at the end of the day, probably a little of both. After all, how much information can you absorb? Let's face it, who we vote for is someone who has our best (or self) interests at heart. Sometimes, these interests get twisted in the wind for votes, and the candidate you thought you were voting for does a back stab for a different segment. Again, in the end, with all the swaying and confusion on the tube, computer, papers, you name it, the odds are most people voted for whom they wanted in spite of the rhetoric which may (or may not) have spewed from their lips.

Sometimes You're the Love Bug, Sometimes You're the Windshield

Any of you listen to both sides of the aisle on news TV regularly? Lately, I've been trying to find the middle, but with everyone on either side not giving credit where it should go, no wonder we suffer. How politicians can argue while Rome continues to burn is beyond belief. I read some blogs from the Ed Show yesterday, and while I do not share many beliefs in his arena, I do understand some basics (you can help real folks suffering in the marketplace from lack of work). Having said that, to simply blame one party or the other for 100 percent of the concerns in this country since the dawn of time is amazing.

If the lame duck congress gets nothing done, well, see above about lame duck feelings here. If Repub's don't do anything in the next two years except spend their time trying to make Mr. Obama look bad, well, that's pretty disingenuous as well. Bailout damage control, state government problems, unemployment, secrets leaking out, the economy, wars, using tax payer funds so unions can benefit from a GM stock sale…the list goes on. Geeze, it's no wonder you can feel like the love bug (Florida folks know what I mean).

Anyway, I will be taking a little time away with the kids/grandkids for some fun in the islands for a few days…sometimes, it feels good to be the windshield.

And now…the News

Well, I'm back. Ok, let's see. Oh yeah, first, the airports. It's real simple boys and girls; first, you remove all the metal from your person you can (apologies to the entire pace maker folks out there); next, you walk through the machine, and presto! You get to put your shoes back on and away you go. Now, if you either forget to do these things or by chance, something on you does set the machine off, then you have two choices. Pats downs and/or body scans. I saw one or two folks going through this stuff and they did it. If you are one of those who will object, well then, I suppose that's why they call it America. Do your objecting if you wish, just be out of most other folks' way.

Next we have the wonderful world of technology. I had a little time for a Bloody Mary so I sat in the waiting area (bar too full) and did what I do besides read; that is, observe. Some of us like to, but I believe it is a dying art. In my immediate seating area, NO ONE was looking up from whatever electronic device they were using. I kid you not. As I scanned a little further from my area, mostly all were in the technology zone. It's a shame. No talking, no…"chit-chat" with folks who may be nice but never meet again. Some day we won't require bodies to get to where we go since all we do is look at the screens. No sense going anywhere so the body will just dry up. It really must piss some people off that unless the wire is sticking out of their ears, what they'll miss between walking to flights, obtaining their baggage, shutting the kids up, etc. anyway, you get the idea.

When I did hear about some news, it was mostly ugly. I hear about a football player who won't play on certain downs (meaning for either a running or passing play for the few of you not inclined to follow the game"). The player or players won't show up for certain practices, whether required or otherwise. They won't speak to their coaches. I suppose the next thing is not playing if the temperature gets too hot or cold, or maybe if the stadium is outdoors or real instead of artificial turf. I don't know if said participants will ever read this from here, but you must be kidding. You make, I don't know, what the gross national product is of half the countries in the world in a year or three and for this; you believe you're bigger than the game? A lot of big babies out there. I realize you life as a player may not be as long as a working stiff in the real world, but hey, after a few years, you'd think you would have enough sense as an adult to save some of that dough the owners feel so compelled to pay. Must've been real fun pampering the hell out of these kids when they were growing. There were days....never mind....the pendulum...it does seem to swing slow sometimes.

The banks, the banks, oh, how they cry for more bailout dough, while the soldier gets a pay cut. Real great example there, government and you wall street whiz kids. Your experiments in this last great go around really cost us. The banks need more free money to plow back into guaranteed deals (no money for you, soup nazi). I mentioned to K the other day if a wall street type thought he/she could make another million bucks for themselves on the backs of others hard work, should the worker lose what the market has done to his/her meager savings, so be it. I would like to believe fewer people like this exist today...but I cannot. These type of folks do not qualify under the "don't envy the rich, don't pity the poor" category. Of course, there are some exemplary cases, and to those, I applaud and congratulate, for they are true patriots.

I believe the plane's taking us on, so off we go.

"Awesome" and "Good Job"

I will probably hit a nerve here. In my day of childishness, doing something your little brain should do just should be done. I was "five across the backside" if you didn't listen too well. I won't advocate those methods, as sometimes in our growing experiences, we know not what we do. However, as in pendulum theory, how far we have come. Don't you parents, caregivers realize what the little one have figured out? Ok, so when we did ten "good" things (by the way, this is for you adults in your field of endeavor as well, but you probably know this) we received an "atta boy". When that thing which was done caused an "aw shit", well, now you need at least ten "atta's" to make up for the faux pas.

Well, the kids know how to mess with ya'. Their idea is to reverse the above proven theory. They will drive you nuts, not listen, throw tantrums and such, until you finally get them to do something nice, what they should be doing anyway, but nice. Then you say one of those "nice job/awesome" things to them, and in their little devilish minds, one nice "atta" gets you another ten or more "aw's". By the way, if you are looking for an alternative to these five across the behind or atta's/aw's situations, I don't really have one. Just deal with it as best you can.

Other than that, buy low, sell high, watch the gas prices fly.

The Gods must like crazy people...He makes so many of us

I realized I mentioned this topic earlier above, but it surfaces again. Anyone following the electric car rush-to-own scenario must be going crazy trying to figure out the logic. Look, I know it would just be as fun as jumpin' into a bag of rattle snakes to own one, showing off your "pc ness", but hell, can you figure out what the hell they're talking about?

I mean, one car gets the equivalent of 137 miles to the "gallon" of gas, I assume, but can only get you 40 miles or so down the road. Then the competition says they can get 235 miles to said gallon, but only 72 miles or so on the charge. These incredible statistics will be a real comfort to me while I'm stuck on the Overseas Highway missin' my first "Pain-In-The-Ass" cocktail at Holiday Isle in the Keys.

I realize this type of vehicle is not yet ready for the long haul, but guys, come on, how crazy do we have to be to buy into these numbers, all for the incredibly low job lost, inflation every rising, unemployment check covering cost of in the $35-40 thousand dollar range? Oh, I forgot the charger, in your garage (not on the turnpike yet), for another $3-4 thousand. And, do not forget the cost of electricity, which I am certain, will be much cheaper to you once you set up those solar panels or grids in your house. But don't worry; you'll get a tax credit which should recover the cost in say, a gazillion years.

If you want the car, don't concern yourself about making a statement, for those who do may be superfluous. Buy it and use for its intended purpose, to go to the grocery store. Some day, it may be the thing to do, but for now, if you believe we're going to run out of fossil fuels in the near term…buy it or walk.

December 11, 2010

The holiday season is in full bloom. Karen's in the workroom attending to her embroidering wares. It's a frustrating day, and those of you who venture into the small business arena understand these things. She has received an earful about the benefits of capitalism from none other than son-in-law. I am grateful for the advice to her (since it has echoed mine prior) and I believe she is as well, although we are who we are, and with everything else on her plate, maybe it's not yet time to cut into your investments for money. Maybe it will come soon, maybe next year, but as we, the ordinary folks get older, I wonder if there will be an ability to "trip the trigger" and go for the profit incentive. No matter how it turns out, it will be for the best.

I take leave now to catch up on the latest books out there, and have a cigar down by the water with scotch, hoping the aroma catches the colonel's sniffer, so as to recap about the week's endeavors.

Sometimes, I really Have Nothing in the Tank

Not that I haven't collected fodder for upcoming thoughts, but they aren't formulated in my head yet. Besides, I know I am going out for an errand or two shortly, and it's very cold (for Florida) out there, so it stymies the mind. You ever notice no matter how warm you try to get on cold days, there are always what I call "cold spots" on your body. Mine are the back or side of my arms and legs at times, but the primary culprits are the toes. No matter that every other body part is comfy, them toes are still a tinglin' and numb. Maybe it's the circulation, I don't know. Anyway, I realize there are some other spots above and ones coming where the words don't seem to come out right or maybe don't even make sense, but it is what it is. Go write a book.

Cycling…the other "White Meat" of the Environmental Circuit

I have nothing against cycling and they probably follow the rules of the road as well as drivers. However, not the ones I see (or you see, if you're reading this). The cyclist races along, comes to a stop sign and, and…. go right through it…after I come to full stop just to see what the cyclist will do. Or take way too much room in the road, especially when there is a perfectly long straight sidewalk when nobody's using it. What is it about not using the side walk? Something in bike lore I don't understand. Is the concrete sidewalk different from an asphalt street? You'd rather be the hit by a car rather than hit a pedestrian? You folks in the vehicles (especially the non-cyclists) know what I mean. According to Florida law (which could be different in other states), a bicycle is defined as a vehicle and subject to the same laws (i.e. traffic lights, stop signs, etc.) as a car. Oh, and in case you were wondering, like K had me doing, a bicycle can be ridden on the sidewalk (subject to local ordinances) and both pedestrians and cyclists have the same rights. However, the bike must yield the right-of-way to a pedestrian and be "audible" signal wise when passing. Good luck with that one.

I agree drivers should be recognizant of opening doors and making turns cutting cyclists off, but as is usually the case, cyclists seem to use the law to take more advantage than should be allowed (like most of the cars in handicapped spaces which really shouldn't be there; how many sports cars in those slots?). Anyway, like the Kid from Brooklyn says "think about it!!!"

Some Dance to Remember, some dance to Forget

All due respect to a classic Eagles tune, I had this problem about this time last year. I don't know, maybe it's the season, maybe not, but there seems to be more time between thoughts and gatherings of the old guys these days. Maybe it's because some of us are departed, maybe not as much time to travel or tougher to make the effort. Maybe it's just my imagination.

Am I alone in this thought process? Is it because we do less because we just don't make the time, or just don't care, or just getting older not to give a damn? In a similar vein, I was talking to K about an idea for the book I was certain I would remember. The recorder wasn't handy, but I thought "how could I forget such a topic which was foremost in my mind?" Well, I forgot it, and not that I tried to remember the next day or so. I mean I forgot it within the hour. I mean... what the hell? What's weird is, it's not the first time. I know, I know, we are all hard wired to remember some things that never go away and some that do, but when you're trying to drive home ideas, issues, etc. well, I wish it were a little easier to remember. Maybe it's just meant to be that way. Let's dance and it won't matter anyway.

Smile for the Camera

So, how much to you truly believe in what you're saying, eh? I watched a couple of congruent news shows yesterday and I wonder about the methodology of people. Well, not really, but if you're voicing some outsized opinion on say, whether you believe there should be Christmas carols sung in the malls, my question would be...in your 50, 60 or 70+ times going around the sun, where were you on these matters until say, the day before yesterday? That would be the day before you were asked to spew your rhetoric about the matter. Don't get me wrong, whether you believe in some idea or otherwise, it's ok...just don't let the camera sway your opinion to the point where "it's really about me, and not the issue".

XMAS

We spoke with my sister today. She sounded and is very tired. There's too much to do with family and folks spread around this time of year. This scenario is repeated around the country of many folks. It's too bad because the businesses, large and small, need to make this time of the year work for them, or many suffer or go away. Speaking for myself, I do not believe in "the time of the year" so much as why we need to change any of our inherent philosophy of how to live our lives.

In the great Depression, everyone around you was in the same boat. Now, if you are hurting without the means to carry on with your lives, all you need is a TV to see everyone else is buying all this stuff (do they really need?) and you are not, so it must just be you. That couldn't be further from the truth. While presents and things may be nice, probably most everything you need or have is all you need to be thankful.

So, Now Where are the Jobs?

This one's going be a good one. The wheel, printing press, light bulb, internal combustion engine, computer, internet…who is going to put the next object forward to make it happen? Not folks like John Deere; heck their going to build plants in China. Not that I can blame them. You can slap that sucker up in no time. No big regulatory requirements or unions or red tape (no pun intended). Not banks, they're too busy paying big fines (out of their slushy sinking funds) to cover up tax dodges they knew they would have to pony up for eventually. Heck, they'll just make it up on the next deal. Not wall street. They're wondering how to keep their bonuses intact. That might keep some hired help for them, but it isn't going to produce any widgets. I wonder if they still use that term in the classroom. Widgets. A fabricated factory with a fabricated balance sheet with fabricated profits (anyone see "Back to School"?). Such one or two dimensional bull.

We need to convince more manufacturing companies to allow factories to be built here. Enough hamburger and paper flipping. Maybe we will. I see where Electrolux decided they would build a factory here instead of Mexico. Bully for them and us. Maybe it's a start. It has to start somewhere.

Everyone is Tied for First

You ever notice in a conversation about prescribing something someone will say "you should go see him/her, he/she's' the best widget maker here"…I realize in some extreme cases this statement could be true, but let's face it; if we think about it, it's merely a statement of opinion, based on personal experiences and/or bias. I like my dentist, my doctor, my broker and my accountant. To say they are the best invites trouble (as a matter of fact, it has on more than one occasion). This type of advice is convenient at times but can have unintended consequences. While I admit to having requested such services in the past, I would be more than wary if someone swore up and down about a particular person's expertise after a certain point. There actually can be times when a lot of servers can be a good thing and choosing ones other than ones recommended can have its merits.

At one point in one person's convenience to location, cost, effectiveness, etc. can work to another person's detriment. This is not to say the recommendation may necessarily be a bad one, just a thought of doing one's own homework at times may serve up a better plate of options.

It Says Ten items OR LESS, DAMMIT!!!

If you are like most guys, if you are the one who does some of the food shopping, you prefer it as early as possible, like when the store employees outnumber the shoppers. Granted, sometimes the things you may want (like some real fresh Cuban or French breads) may not be out, but that's the price you pay for things like no crumb crunchers in your way in the aisles. There's no one in your way when you order some fresh ham. You try this at say, noontime, and the assisted living center buses are in the parking lot (no offense, I could be there anytime myself). Our more senior citizens like to order as much cold cuts as they can while they sample everything at the counter and start gabbing with the lady/man behind the counter. Geez, it's not like I'm in a hurry, but for me, hangin' out at the grocery story is not my idea of slack time.

Then would come the cart battles and the noise and half the stuff you want gone anyway (this is still at the noontime stop by). Then…it happens. The person or persons in front of you at the check out counter can't…make…or…find…their…money (or credit/debit card) while they're on line. If they slide the card, a lot of times, it doesn't work. Then, God forbid, you are in the "ten items or less aisle". It seems this country still has a severe problem with math. What makes it worse is the checker doesn't say anything. There are ten persons <u>or more</u> behind this mathematically challenged person holding up the line while ignoring what they've done. Then, the card won't work, etc, etc. You get the idea. Anyway, if you have to shop, go early; if you're in a pinch, grin and bear it.

Only the Big Five Know for Sure

Today I read the oil companies are about to go crazy exploring for the black gold, Texas tea (for all you Beverly Hillbilly fans). What, no outcry about alternative energies? Of course, the price of oil is going up and we end up paying at the pump. Whether this trend will continue over the next one, two or ten years will be anyone's guess. Housing is once again in the "Thomas A", unless you're a real buyer with no baggage attached from a previous housing debacle. The speculators are out, and all the usual precious metals are in, so this ought to be fun. Err, no, not for you and me you see, because all these guru's and folks who leave their lofty posts in the world to "tell all" now about how bad the next downfall will be, well, they're all heading for the hills or wherever the next hot getaway spot they flock.

My own, previously conceived, thoughts are that only the Big Five know, and they ain't saying where it's all going to head. My broker loves when I spew this stuff; scares the hell out of'em because they probably think I'm nuts and not all worth it for the nickel and dimes I keep tucked away there. In any event, this is another of my opinions that I prefer to stick with, but you are, of course, free to draw your own conclusions.

It's cold out there, Baby

Its quiz time, folks. See if you can get the correct answer.

So everyone seems to be blaming the weather on;

- A. The media- after all, they talk about it so much, you'd believe someone could do something about it;
- B. The airlines-heck, it must be their fault; ever since 1978, they've been deregulating the hell out of everything, so why can't they deregulate the skies?
- C. Airline passengers-they all just want to go home or some other place for the holidays, how come that darn winter just crept up on them without any warning?
- D. Government-well, at least this is a time honored category for blame. While Presidents and governors and congress folks all went home and/or away for this particular time, they were getting back at all those folks who were traveling and didn't vote for them. (You'd think most folks would be glad their representatives were out of town. The corresponding locales probably run just as well if not better when they're not around);
- E. God-my personal favorite. I have no qualms with forces in the universe, but, well, you've got

to be kidding. Whose God, yours religion's, someone else's?

F. All of the above;

G. None of the above.

The answer might surprise you. It's G. The real culprit is…the National Football League. I mean after all, playing a football game on a Tuesday night after a gazillion years or so, you gotta' be testing the weather and the frozen waters from above. If those boys can't play football on that Sunday because of the weather, what chance to you have to travel free of the aggravation you just went through?

I can feel the tongue really sticking into the side of my cheek.

Yaw's Bringing Us off Course

Happy New Year to all. It has been a few since I last wrote, but the last few weeks seem to do that to me. Besides, you probably need to recover from tripping around, hangovers, going back to work if you do that sort of thing. Got to bring the stick back to its upright positioning now.

It's also another excuse for me because even as a write this, I am sort of winging it more than usual. With all the trappings of the season, I just felt the urge to start typing (or Dragon speaking, for those who know and use the verbal word software).

A new government. Wow. With what little I have read about already, some of it will be lame, or stay that way. One of the books I am reading right now is about our first leader, Mr. Washington. I am partially through the book, but I find it fascinating. I try to imagine what it was like to start out on one side (he fought for the British first because that is where the family history is from; in the French and Indian Wars for those of you who are not aware), then go through such a transformation to overcome all odds to start this USA thing rolling.

There are great moments in our history, or maybe I should say turning points as this one (Abraham Lincoln, Louis Armstrong, Babe Ruth and Jackie Robinson, to name a few). If you don't know much about why these folks are pivotal in our history, you should read them, as I have, although I am by no means an expert. I am merely a student who is trying to understand the big picture a little better. I would read the Washington book faster, but it is long and the print much smaller than the font I am using to type here (the book was a gift from Karen, so no Kindle download there).

Maybe it's just because we get older and try to understand a little more about where we came from while you have the time. In my opinion, these were great people, who overcame great injustices, prejudices and maybe, as in Mr. Ruth's case, were in the right place at the right time (a subsequent necessity with talent after the Black Sox scandal). What courage it must have taken to have the character to be the way they were. Not perfect individuals, but ones which were able to transform us for the better at each stage of their place in history.

Lately, it seems we are lacking for the above type of individual. Maybe it's the history, meaning the time is not right for such individuals to arrive, or maybe we will have a collective of very good individuals who will do us right to preserve the union. When the 112th Congress decided to read the Constitution, to me it wasn't whether it was right or wrong to do so, but if you saw the seats in the Congress, as this document was being read, there were not many in attendance. If you believe in the Constitution's "antiquity", then you should strive to change or amend what's on your mind through our procedural jurisprudence, and not because it doesn't fit the needs of a particular judges ruling at the moment. Those are the moments when anarchy rears its ugly head.

You've probably all seen scenarios in the news where certain countries have their respective congresses jumping on each other in fist fights over what they cannot agree. It may seem a little funny at the moment, but do you really want that to happen here? Maybe these great figures are trying to tell us we as individuals can be good and great and collectively strive and evolve to good and great things without the need for heroes?

The "game" goes on, a little battered, betrayed and bruised at times, always surviving, always evolving as part of our ever learning, living process for the better. I believe the yaw's upright at this moment; hope it stays that way.

Will I Cut My Own Throat, at Least a Little?

Discussions abound around cutting deficits from local to federal government balance sheets. You cannot seem to avoid these topics anymore. Ok, ok, so here goes; does anyone think newer appointments to the Congress would consider cutting third rail items?

We've always had hawk and dove issues on how much money the military machine needs, and with the way of the world today, it may need to consider a shifting of funds from some supposed defensive postures to more of a protectorate one, with our borders becoming more a priority.

Then of course, there are the "grey" areas of social security and Medicare. I don't know what's so "social" about it, seeing as how the topic can get so confrontational, but I digress. Let's say a young up and comer to the world of Washington decides to make this a topic for serious discussion with the rank and file there. Obviously, it would be prudent to believe a certain segment of the voting population would not consider cutting any benefit toward this program. There were times in our past when government health care and privatizing social security had risen, to be met with even more resound to defeat these measures. Of course, many of us believe the time was still not right to bring the issue of government "sponsored" health care up again, but this time it gets by. Not because of any real voting ideologies brought on by Congress, but because some folks believe we can trash the Constitution whenever it suites our needs to slide things by the

American people. That discussion is still in debate and with the present Congress, some adjusting may come about, but for that we will just have to wait and see.

The Social Security course to privatize also seems to have picked the wrong time in our history to attempt this change. Admittedly, had it occurred during the Bush administration, some disastrous results may have occurred due to the recent economic situation. Further, we understand folks using this safety net for most if not their entire not so "golden years" at times may not have the ability or many more trips around the sun to recover from such a malady.

You see elderly people outside a government office with picket signs about not bankrupting the country for their kids/grandkids and such, but don't consider changing their habits when it comes to Social Security? As much as it would at least nick my own throat, these are issues which need to be addressed and amended. Your elected representatives may stress the need for the safety net, but since they squandered the funds which were not used for their originally intended purpose, what's the harm in controlling your own destiny, at least a little? Unscrupulous brokers? Been there and that will never change. Change the rules/penalties and send'em to jail, period. Too old to make correct decisions in the market? That's hogwash. You can make simple good decisions about where the money you earned can go. You're older, not dead. Once again, I stress the 100 percent rule, which is; there ain't any such thing or guarantee. We've tried with the gatekeepers in Washington to control it all, and it didn't work.

At least in theory, give the new guy and gals a chance to make the changes necessary to promote a better country. I figure it's better than what's happened to the money to date.

I Get an "Out" for Everything

I was giving a soap box discussion speech in the vehicle yesterday to K. when, after fully explaining a situation, totally feeling in the right, said "but of course, I could be wrong". Sometimes I will remember to say this simply because I am making an attempt to emphasize that I am not wrong, but mostly, "but I could be wrong".

That's the way it is when you can ultimately challenge yourself into believing in everything you say and think you know, then believe in none of it. It's weird, I know, but some of you may understand. I hope I am not going down the George Soros lane. I will not attempt to argue the finer points about Mr. Soros' past to present. Safe to say, if you read any history about him, there seems to have been some decent things done early on, then the world or he changed, maybe because he thought he could with all the wealth attached to the thought process. Anyway, the point I was trying to make was, there were influences in Mr. Soros' life which, according to research, led him to believe in fallibilism. This is a belief that all knowledge gained by someone could be wrong, or that it is impossible to believe any idea could be 100 percent accurate.

You may admit there are times when this ideology can come in handy, but aside from the obvious problem of who's ever right, Yo' Mr. S, if you believe in this "out", are you going to give back the money? Of course, it's a convenient out when you need one I suppose, and this philosophy has been believed by several thinkers over time. I do not profess to have ever run into someone who is a believer, but then again, I don't get out much.

I could believe in the "fallibilistic" viewpoint of suddenly not understanding something we thought we had previously completely understood through any additional educational process. A lot of us don't want "hardwired" views of the world, earned possibly over many years through careers and study, having to be turned upside down. The continuing process of learning or adapting to new ideas or even different ones if not so new cannot be such a bad thing. My father (God bless his soul) likes to say he is too old learn anything new. If that's the attitude you want to take, it's a point. If it's one you don't, well then, we can grow from our mistakes, misgivings or predetermined set of ways to evolve. I think I've been down this road before, so you get the point. Then of course, I could be wrong.

Poem Time

For all you Bill O'Reilly fans out there, and maybe those who aren't;

William is a fellow, who likes to volley,

Who informs all as he can, most rightly,

I attempt in my folly, to write a book like O'Reilly,

But nothing stirs even close to Bill's almighty

It came to me, what else can I say?

Less than average

Lately, due to circumstances, I have found myself feeling a little apprehensive, frustrated and downright angry. The words are hard to come by without these feelings and I am trying not to cross the boundaries set by myself. The state of affairs from personal, professional and governmental perspective (that being my perspective of government) has become more difficult to understand. By this I mean more government intrusion, more potential taxation in an event starve off budgetary woes created by the very institution of individuals who started this intrusion in the first place. A pet peeve of mine is in the area of military dissatisfaction for those who need assistance the most. It seems when politicians and their offshoots have problems it hits the limelight with such irreverence they believe everyone should be aware of their concerns and misgivings and unfortunate happenstance on a consistently daily basis. While I certainly do not wish any ill will against any other human being, when military personnel are sent to do the bidding of these politicos, sometimes they come home in worse shape than they left. While they have to transverse through the VA's network of trials and tribulations to resolve personal matters, either from a physical, mental or financial standpoint, these can be greater hurdles then the ones they were sent out to protect and defend. The damage created here does a disservice to these individuals and to the country as well. I don't know what as individuals we can do about much of this matter. Other than seeing the occasional service man or woman being honored at a halftime football game, most with issues have to go on with their lives struggling at times to put the pieces back together on their own with little or no help from the very institution that asked them to serve.

I need to review these words when I am a little more coherent in my thoughts but I wanted to put them down so I could make the determination which of these potentially stinging statements should be left for the few of those who may ultimately read them, give them some thought and think that I'm crazy or otherwise. I may leave most of it as is. I believe the camaraderie between those individuals who serve do it because of a sense of patriotism and for their brothers in arms. I believe these reasons exceed any sense of loyalty to others especially those who make the laws in these times for these individuals to follow. I don't feel very eloquent in my thought process here and the words may not seem to make much sense at times but it is how I feel at this moment. I truly hope that I will give cause to feel differently at some point when it is proven these feelings are repairable and mistaken.

I believe many of these fine folks only wish to do what is expected of them to the best of their abilities, come home after their time is served and function as normal everyday productive human beings to the best of their respective abilities. Anything less is considered a travesty and an insult to the integrity and sacrifices of these fine folks.

The King of Nothing

Regards to Seals and Croft's title (along with "Yellow Dirt", the only other song I really liked) doncha' just feel that's the way it is sometimes. You have so little control of events surrounding you; sometimes it's all a blur. I used to think we are given too much information to attempt to digest on a 24/7 basis. Now I know it. There's just some things you just don't have to bother with to make it through the day, week or live to be happy and go along. Karen was clicking the gum she was chewing in the car the other day and I never thought to mention she sounded like she was trying out for a part in one of those jersey shore sit com's or whatever they call them. Honestly, I draw the line a lot sooner than most on what I will watch of the 300 or so channels available (I truly believe I could live with 5 or 6). To think I even thought of that knowing I wouldn't watch stuff like that on a bet was amazing. You can't escape it. What a societal breakdown. Who thinks that's funny, or even good? I suppose enough folks to keep it going until the next show takes its place.

For me, I'll just go in the back, roll around in the yellow dirt while looking up at the sky, with the thought of being the king of nothing not being so bad.

Progress

A boy growing up in an inner city was enjoying the simple things of youth. Baseball or stickball in the summer, football in the fall, playing all mostly in the streets or sidewalks, snowball fights in the winter. A typical city kid, more than occasionally reprimanded for some of the things boys do in the springtime of their lives. There would always be promises and penance to redeem oneself to priests, parents and police men alike, only to violate those promises again.

In the spring of one's life, one takes full advantage. It's what's natural. School, while important, is secondary to living after school. School would seem to last forever in a day, and when it broke for the summer, would seem to rival for forever time itself.

In the spring of one's life, the opposite sex is…unimportant (unless they could beat you at something important…no, not in school though, school didn't count…girls were always better there).

Being mischievous heightened one's senses to the environment yet it taught you little outside your enclosure domain. What I mean is, "everyone lives like this, don't they?"

Everyone lives in a different time from others, and it was no exception. In this particular time, one would walk to and from school, cross streets yourself or with a friend. You could always play outside in the streets unsupervised, even after dark. When it was time to eat, your mother would yell out the window from six stories above and somehow, no matter where you were at the moment, you always heard her. Time to get going now, or the next call would come from Dad (if he was home from work) and you really didn't want that to occur.

The times didn't seem to go by so fast; until they were gone. You didn't say "I wished I'd done this or that" because well, for our limited understanding of the world, we did everything we'd set out to do. You just started to wonder, what's next?

The world changed fast at the next level because it really became our first understanding of change since the first day of kindergarten (no preschool stuff back then). The adolescent level included more work at home from school, less tolerant teachers, it seemed, because no one was there to hold your hand when you had one of you weaker moments. Included in this time where the "girl-friend" years. Oh, the god-awful truth of life was beginning to affect you; you actually began to think girls weren't so bad (or at least that was what you hormones were saying).

Before you know it…WHAM!!...you're living in New Jersey!! You realized the close proximity to all those taller buildings growing up in the city was no longer the norm, and another point on the good side, the mischievous deeds which, shall we say, the police would've expressed interest, are no longer in your thought process.

So off you go at the "insistence" of your folks to the land of green; a garden state. No more solid concrete areas overlapping endlessly ad nausea. No more sparks from the subway el trying to leap into your bedroom window, yep, the good life now. The "girlie" days (or wars at times) get more interesting, and man, I do Wanna' do a little more than Hold Your Hand…You fill some of the void by taking up hobbies, playing sports or music.

Of course, the stakes are higher. You don't want to piss off the wrong friend, girl or teacher, not necessarily in that order. Friends are friends, so one way or another, you could work that out. Girls have a way about'em, so the safe bet is to try and have more than one show promise or real interest. The teachers, well, they could make or break the grade between a decent post high school challenge, trade school or the draft. It's your call.

It is at this juncture you realize you ain't a kid anymore and, depending on one's psyche, have various ups and downs dealing with this period in one's travels through life. It seems doubtful you can fully adapt to the situation as quickly as you'd prefer, but somehow you realize the capability is there and so you arrive, the new fresh young adult.

The responsibilities of a lifetime are thrust upon one, balancing an education, potential recruitment and a new adaptation to one's yet to be realized full potential. For most, though opportunities abound, it doesn't end with any steady or meteoric rise to the top of one's chosen field of talent; merely a hard working, more hours than you care to remember tortoise's pace's rise to somewhere between the rank and file and the upper end of one's endeavors. A job well done and proud. Of course, one's moral, political, religious and financial ambitions (and again, not necessarily in that order nor all of the aforementioned ambitions) may play a more than minor part in the journey. Hopefully during the processing of one's desires, there will be as few a tragic end attributed to these weaknesses as possible. Hopefully, the desire to avoid the "evils" of society that will accompany some of us will be triumphed by those who can accept the consequences and rewards of a life as best as possible toward themselves and their fellow beings. Oh, and it helps to save a little dough for the proverbial "rainy day"; they come, and it will help, believe me. Not one to give advise (one is only looking for an accomplice when they seek it), the money saving thing is paramount. Should the time arise when offspring add to the fruits of one's labors, they too will learn a good lesson from those who came before.

Some will always prosper more than others, but the strength of being an individual, with all the rights, privileges and opportunities afforded us should always endure.

Did You Ever…..

…notice how the piece of butter you wanted out of the tub is never quite the size you wanted so you end up fighting with the tub to cut the right size?..

…sit out back smokin' a 'gar when your special other comes by sits down and the smoke starts blowing in her/their direction?

…realize the cat is always on the wrong side of the door…

…see how when you empty household trash from one bag to another for convenient throw away, the receiving bag never stays open enough so you always get some (usually the most gooey parts) on the floor…

…read about how in the trials and tribulations of the Father of Our Country (if I have to tell you who that is, stop now, go to the library or Internet and find out), the Continental Congress (there's a hint) and various political bodies of the time thought the soldiers were squandering and being treated well enough. They thought these same soldiers weren't doing their jobs in the cold winter months of the war even thought the British did not historically clash with their foes during these times as much as in the warmer seasons. As if these politicos really understood what it was like to fight for their country in this way (I merely mention this now because I am reading another quality researched history book; not like the ones you and I read in school) and the similarities…..well, you would have to understand what it was like to fight in these conditions, and we better not ever have to find out…

…notice how when you get a slice of ham or cheese out of the package you bought, then try to close said package, the very edge of the plastic paper on the inside of the package always seems to get in the way of zipping the bag closed? Oh, and zipping the bag's an event to challenge your patience as it is!!....

…get all the Pez candies in the dispenser without having the refills explode in your hand and get on the floor….and when you do get them in the dispenser, you can only find eleven of them…the one that's missing goes to some Pez heaven account; maybe so you can use for money when you get there (assuming that's the direction you'd be heading)…

…wonder why all these states fighting for their union rights ever thought about how the money would continuously flow to them without knowing how? In my position in a previous life, the camaraderie exhibited between us as individuals is what got us through the rough spots and where able to act cohesively without depending on outsiders for our daily bread. I suppose it's too late for that for the dwindling union populace, but when you always want your leaders to fight you battles, your leaders are the ones who get the most wampum…

…notice how three days after you finish a painting chore around the house, and at least three or four showers later, while you're reading a book or watching the tube, you manage to still find a speck or two of paint on your finger or arm?

…notice how the itch is always just out of reach?

….when you want to turn from the front page of any newspaper to continue reading on page "A12" you will always get to the pages in between real easy but have wet your fingers like crazy to reach A12?

…wonder when I would stop this (or any) particular section of the book?

"Boy the way Glen Miller played"

Karen's been getting on me lately about the writing. You see, I have been dragging thought wise of late. Sure, there seems to be plenty to discuss, but it just hasn't rung the bell, so to speak. You all hear about how this country's trying to be bankrupted out by those who believe we can still print money like their lining up to buy it. That party can change; just ask any historian or economist who is unbiased (if that's possible). It's the same old rhetoric and we don't seem to be doing enough to…think about…well…us.

By "us", I mean the United States of America. Too many politicos seemed to have sold us out a long time back, and I don't know if it's possible to change. I really like some of the changes in our lives which technology has brought forth, but somewhere along the way, we let too much go awry… ("songs that made the hit parade…)

I read an article in today's paper about the government's cost overrun agencies (now, here I go; K's got me writing when I still didn't seem in the mood). The numbers aren't exact, and I don't wish to get up to check them, but 56 agencies checking on…on…I changed my mind; I wanted to get it right...82!!...that's it…82 federal agency programs to improve teacher qualify. Who the hell are we kidding? I think if I saw more than one, it would be freaky. Then 80 more for the "disadvantaged"…what the hell is that? The 56 number I got in my head above was for programs to help people understand finances. For the finances I am thinking about, a whole slew of us could educate folks under one program for a whole lot less.

Look, we've always assumed these tragedies with the taxpayer's money, but when you see it in print…I am sorry, but it's not their money, so there is no accountability. I cannot make it any clearer. When the government was closer to balancing the budget and occasionally getting there in the old days, boy it sure must've felt good ("guys like us we had it made").

There's more to the story, but why bother? I don't wish to contribute to the overburdened medical professions' problems with another old guy in the system for a heart attack. I will take another "Fukitole" and think of how some things have changed for the good, but still sometimes, not ("those were the days").

Oil Everywhere

So, how many of you believe the Chinese and the Russians will be kinder to the Caribou and the spotted speckled three legged Pekinese triple breasted snow bird? I am looking…I don't see many hands a' waiving here.

Here's my answer. Start digging and drilling…NOW. Or yesterday, if you prefer. Technology will come, but…not…NOW. Or yesterday, if you still prefer. Electric this, and solar that, it's all wonderful and we should embrace it, but again, if you believe the Chinese and Ruskies are concerned about their carbon footprint while they make deals with other nations to provide or import energy, you need to save every penny and book onto that hotel "they" are making in space soon. Maybe stay there until they try to kick you out, then whaddatheygonnado'…shoot you into space? We will always care for wildlife in some way, shape or form better than the aforementioned geographies. It may not be perfect, but if we're not around to continue our way of life, well, then that's it…Poof! We're gone.

You will probably still be driving an internal combustion engine by the time you read this (wishful thinking on my part…the reading of this that is). Would you prefer to pay $6-8, maybe $10.00 a gallon some day, or something a little less, simply because it is shipped from a closer source? Do you really believe mother Earth will die because of all the extra harm drilling will bring to it or that those "greedy-grubby" oil conglomerates will make even more of the killing they make now, even if it means cheap energy to you?

That's the problem with us…we get mad about what everyone else is doing so much we don't mind our own store. Keep it simple, keep it local, and everyone's locale will take care of itself. I believe local governments can run better than state ones and state ones better than federal ones. Keep voting in the ones you need, out with the ones you don't, and well take back our country…now…or yesterday, if you prefer.

…And furthermore…

In a previous life, I was involved with a business which banks, thinking our existence was no less than nefarious, called us "the dark side". It's all pretty hilarious when you consider it's the banks, at least the more notable ones, who seem to cry the loudest. They get the best deals on lending dough, and then screw that up, try to get into your business, screw things up even more. Then, when there's no more business to be had, they cry to the government for your money, expect…no, demand they be bailed out, only to brag about making some money on the backs of the taxpayers. What a farce.

We had no such protection. We lived with our errors, trudged through the bad times and didn't overly reward ourselves simply because it looked like we would have a good day, week, month or year. If you saw how many people would qualify for the "by today's standard's" lowly amount of bonus pool money to make the cut at the branches, you would laugh. All of our stock options were restricted; that is to say you could only exercise small portions over several years so the incentive to do well was ever present. And so, what do the banks/brokerages do when things seem to not be so bad, overly reward again...that's it; party like it's 1999…..

You think maybe, we shouldn't let them fail, that how many jobs and related businesses would be affected by this; I say let'em fail. The business which continually gets the hand out and knows they will continue to do so operate most inefficiently. Those jobs should be lost to others who want and can perform well. You keep paying the wrong people the most money, and you get the red ink that seems to permeate in these areas as well as Washington. This may sound a little bitter, but I assure you, it is not. I have had enough time away from said former life to think about the aforementioned doctor's office visits to laugh it off. As someone once gave me an old Latin proverb, "Illegitimus Noncarborundum" –"don't let the bastard's grind you down".

Ok, K's just got home; time to get off the bitch stand again.

Fait accompli

Well, we folks here in Florida won't be getting a "high speed" train any time soon, at least not with Fed dough. I may be in the minority here, but I for one am glad. First, these things bring mostly temporary (albeit needed) jobs at best. Second, as an old hand at riding subways, buses and trains way back, they do not run profitably and eventually get subsidized by you and me. This will occur, no matter what the politicians say, so the ones that push and scream for these things have an agenda of which we are not aware (I bring to your attention South Florida Tri Rail, already being subsidized by the taxpayers for some 35 million dollars or so). They will overstate, no, grossly overstate ridership, and unless you want to go down the mandate line, we'll be sorry. We will not reinvent the wheel here. Third, it will cost more to go from point "A" to point "B" or "C", or whatever letter you're trying to get to…simply because it cannot get you close enough. They are not going to be built where they should go. Yeah, yeah, you get a few less cars on the road, what with gas prices moving like jumping beans, but if the price of fuel goes to new permanent type highs, you think the price of a ticket's going to stay the same?

Finally, and mostly, since I have asked K about this, did the people not vote on this matter a few times over the last several years, and did they not turn it down? Just another example of elected officials not listening to their constituents, I suppose.

We can use the money for more permanent solutions in the infrastructure, which lead to more permanent jobs. Any state that takes our rejected funds should be ashamed, no?

Just Another Day

I am at the service station for another oil change. Does anybody call it a "service station" anymore? The owner, whom I have known for over thirty years, informs me he's a little behind this morning with setting up shop for the day. He goes out of the main office area we are in, checks on the service bays and comes back into the office to say he's got a bay for me. Pretty boring stuff, eh? Yep, that's the way it goes sometimes and of late, but I really don't mind.

I think we take being bored as being a little lazy or unproductive. Not me. I realize that obtaining what I believe to be the necessity of boredom is a lost art. You cannot place enough importance of this event. With major topics of energy, earthquakes countries on the brink and the struggles of our own situation, and who wants to sacrifice some of what they think they deserve but expects everyone else to cooperate in that regard. All these things can keep one up at night or walk around during the day in a zombie like state.

We go about taking yoga or karate or meditate; all things to help us escape, when the easiest thing to do is to be bored. I do not mean the type of boredom that says "I am not busy and nothing is sparking my interest" type. I mean while I sit waiting for the car to be serviced, I am looking out the window at the sky or cars or people and be happy I am sitting here able to comprehend being alive. I am not on the cellular, not texting or tweeting or whatever your "fingered choice" prefers. These are just pure old "good to be alive on the rock" thoughts (K's really gonna' think I've lost it here). I am not taking any medication, honest, except when the "Fukitols" are necessary.

I may have gone down this road a few times. I don't mind waiting for the oil change. No quickie zippidy-do oil change store for me. It's a nice day. When the car is really, I think I'll take a drive, stop along the way to smell the weeds, and listen to the sounds of everyday life. The ultimate of boredomness.

As Good as You Are…As Bad as I Am…

You know, it's pretty amazing. I received an online copy of the latest magazine from a friend that relates to my former life. In it, I find it very intriguing how things come full circle. Now I realized some of the methodology and financing aims towards what type of funding they do has changed a little, but let me give you some short quotes or quips, if you may.

"Changing times require new approaches"…well, that's original…

"Each funder's business model may require a different approach, we felt that a common sense, bottom line approach works best…I assume they mean a profitable bottom line, but again, if you have to explain to someone that common sense goes hand and hand with profits….

"The economy forced us to reinvent ourselves"…I certainly hope so or this interview is over…

"We saw an opportunity because banks and finance companies were not lending to small and medium sized companies"…if I had a nickel for ever time I heard that…

"They (the customer) might have had a bankruptcy in their past and not doing as well as they were a few years back (I assume before the bankruptcy), but they still have assets of value. We lend against that value with less regard for how they're doing financially"…better get a Lo-Jack or some other device attached to you equipment bud, because it when it leaves point "A", it ain't comin' back…

I have paraphrased in all these instances, but you understand. Don't get me wrong. I applaud those companies who do survive to accomplish whatever end game they are trying to achieve, and if it means sometimes catch phrases are the best you can do from the sixties or seventies, what the hell. I just find it a bit amusing. One company thought it would be good to rewrite bank loans because the bank didn't want to, and then offered an additional line of credit because the finance company thought they needed it. That's nice, but if they don't go to term, will they invoke the "they forced this money on us" defense? Maybe the paperwork protects, I don't know.

If these different companies can employ folks and give some hope to the future of small businesses, then it's a good thing. They might as well. No matter what the banks say about their lending practices in the media, most of these businesses don't stand much of a chance obtaining funds any other way. The funding sources themselves have to keep reinventing themselves so they can obtain the necessary lines of credit and working capital funds. Banks just think they can ignore this business, knowing papa government will bail them out again. These new leasing finance companies would still be considered the "dark side" to the banks, as they did to us in my time.

It reminds of an old Irish toast;

"Here's to you, as good as you are;
 Here's to me, as bad as I am;
 As good as you are, as bad as I am;
 I'm as good as you are, as bad as I am…

…Don't Forget the Credit Unions…

While we are or were on the subject of bailouts, the credit unions want to sue the major brokerage houses for what I call "ill-be-gotten-losses". What, you say, don't you mean gains? Well, yes the regular nomenclature would dictate gains in that saying, but because they were losses, they too, want a "save" from their own ignorance about things in which they had no business investing.

If the brokerages mislead the credit unions, and I have no doubt they did to some extent, then shame on them. But let's face it, the unions, like many state and local governmental agencies in charge of creating wealth to pay for services, were unequipped to understand the complexities of these types of securities. Pride, ego and/or not being able to admit to one's lack of expertise in an area would play a more major reason in this debacle, but then again, it's not the first time these reasons could be used to say a bit of malfeasance was also involved. It's the Peter Principle effect…always growing to one position higher than our abilities….

In any event, the lawsuits will fly, and lawyers on both sides will fire their nukes, and the shit bake that becomes the finished product is more fees for you and me. Never let a good lawsuit go to waste. You and I make mistakes, claim ignorance, go down the dumbfounded road, and have to lick our wounds and go on. Use any word starting with "mis" (mis-taken, mis-calculated, mis-remembered and the all important mis-stress) and I am certain these fine upstanding officials will claim it.

Never let a good Earthquake go to Waste

All due respect and console to those who face extreme suffering in the aftermath, I wonder why these "predictors of the faith" come from out of the blue in an effort, like actors, politicians and media folk, to hawk their wares. They effectually say, "This is God's wrath", evoke a December 21, 2012 prescription for disaster, and I have to wonder; who's God? What God allows for the needless suffering of others while soothsayers predict doom?

I may have mentioned in a previous script a book I had read mentioned that when those who say man was created in God's image…we may have got that backward. In my own limited experience with the Great One, I found it to be a little humiliating and just plain ridiculous at times. Look, I have no problems with anyone doing their thing religious wise, but when folks try to tell you any secularization of your beliefs can't be a private thing, I cannot go there. The wars, the history of this area is too vast for the context of my limited scope and understanding. I wonder when some folks get on their knees they are thanking God for being where and what they are, or are there alternative motives. Any recent movies or depictions of the wars between science and religion is purely coincidental, and should in no way reflect upon the belief of those in charge of these productions. Sure. If you believe that, the movie won't make money or maybe the parting of the Red Sea or Ten

Commandments was just one of those things. The battle between technology and religion is ongoing, with each wanting the upper hand. Everyone asks for forgiveness in their own ways, and if you want to pass along your beliefs to your children or others, that is certainly your prerogative. Just don't be surprised if they don't see it that way or your way, so accept them for what they are.

Stage 7; From Apathy to Dependence

There is the body named Congress;

Who thought they could bring us some Progress;

They fought and they fought,

Maybe all for naught,

And we end up with bupkiss.

Someone reminded me awhile back that the plural word for baboon is a "congress of baboons"…food for thought.

Fight the Good Fight

It's been a few weeks, although you can't tell since I don't use the dates in the titles, but it has been awhile. Nothing excites. It's just the way it is sometimes. The dates in the first "Diary" indicate this but I decided to hide better this time. Things happen in one's life which take over the day-to-day operations of carbon based units.

Done some fixing up stuff, built duck houses for the lake (the ducks are actually using them!). Feel like a proud assist there. There are more grandkids on the way (not sure about that feeling, but none of my business anyway). There are the realities of K's imminent retirement and the struggle and realities of getting a small business off the ground. It's life, and that's all you can say about it.

Fight the good fight….every day.

With thanks to Triumph; a semi-decent song.

Beware of the Prophet seeking (your) Profits

I am having a below average day but decided to drift into bitch land for a moment, rather than let it go and lose all thought of the matters at hand. More soothsayers (and you know who they are these days) condemning the masses under the guise of "helping" those in most need. Hope those in the know who have the ability to peek behind the political/financial/moral curtain sober up long enough to expose what is really going on here.

Getting small groups to rally against the "lazy" large groups who will refuse at some point soon to cater to their egregious needs will come back to bite the

politicos in their head-for-the-hills collective asses.   I
believe once again, we have got this backwards.
While there will always be exceedingly greedy folks
out there with no agenda other than the enhancement
of their needs, supporting the laziness of those really
at fault will, or is, coming to haunt us. What was it I
heard about a saying one time….politicians (and
pundits) greed disguised as servitude, I believe is how
it went.

I mention this even at the expense of the market
gains by those (including myself) who have less of a
problem buying basic needs and figuring out how to
transport themselves without going bankrupt. There
are those who will proclaim the rich should pay more,
but the term "rich" is relevant in relation to who makes
the statement…

Eventually, we can come to realize the price many will
pay to those who do not cast out their efforts to try
and do better. The level of who ends up at the bottom
becomes too broad a category in the hearts and
minds of those in charge, and the charlatans then
come out of the wood work to prey.

I believe many prophets have come before to spew
this rhetoric and better than those we have now. To
continuously drape those with free and subsidized
assistance will surely lead to our demise. Maybe
that's old and said before, but maybe it needs to be
constantly said because we're not good at
remembering. Those who can pay more, maybe they
should and probably do of their own free will as much
as their consciousness allows. However, as I may
have mentioned before, those that can skirt

unreasonableness have the ability to do so and will do it.

It can be proven even if we took all the wealth of the nation, that to include all monies earned by individuals and corporations, eliminated all the tax breaks and had 100% taxation, you may solve the problem…for a year. Then what? The wealth is gone, but the debt (not to mention to incalculable unemployment drama) still remains. There's nothing left to tax because there is no economy. Money is worthless and lest we forget, that gold's sure not gonna' taste good in your mouth.

The Scourges of the Earth

Remote controls, mini vans and malls….need I say more. Let's face it, if remote control was never invented, we'd be considerably less weighty, no? Still, too late, enjoy the remote. Mini vans, well, need I say more? Whose idea was that anyway? What a nerdy looking thing no matter who makes it? People like to blame cell phones, texting, putting on makeup in the car because you're late for work due to fender benders (or worse). Not me. It's those mini's, while you're trying to drive and the little ones are just out of smacking reach because they're too busy fighting over what movie to watch instead of enjoying Mother Earth…anyway, they're still ugly. Malls, go to the local grocery or small outlet, support your town, stay off the highways at least until the gas can be bought without taking out a loan. Ride your bike to the store (with or without helmets, geeeze, you'd think we were invalids with these getups they wear…folks, it's LIFE, no guarantees, go have a little cheap fun and enjoy!)

More Scourges in the Fine Print

Is everyone just sick and tired of the fine print on the television commercials? You know, K saw something on a cell phone commercial the other day and it reminded her to check something out on the invoice we receive. She thought about how long it would take before the I-pad commercials would get to her. I asked if she really thought she needed one, or has the commercial done its job (stop me if you'd heard this before). That is to state; the purpose of a commercial, at least a successfully one, is to make you feel like you're the only one in the world who does not own the product or service.

In my former life, many clients did not enjoy fine print items which they did not understand. They understood the risks of borrowing, but did not like the creditor friendliness of the documentation. Sometimes I could not blame them, but they understood the risks and when things didn't work out, well, you'd have bankrupt customers trying to sue you under the RICO act. Yet on the tube (or flat screen) you see fine print all the time so what's the beef? Caveat emptor; let the money plop per downer beware and know that everything has a risk factor.

Final Thoughts-Lessons I Already Knew but Sometimes Forget

Political correctness can be defined as media hype wanting to continually introduce the "eeewwww" factor and peel another layer of skin. My advice to those who adhere to this philosophy…grow a set.

Remember; when you lose sight of your true goals and path, you will surely go down the wrong one and stop working like you don't need the money. Shareholder value is bunk without customer and employee concerns.

Anyone care for a prediction that if we continue the way we are going as a whole in this country, only the privileged and the suck-ups will survive, both corporately and personally. Maybe that's the way it will go and folks will be satisfied, but know that the laws and rules which invoke promises to those mentioned above can easily be changed and you find yourself on the other side of the fence.

No, my friends, the Founding Fathers were not perfect (you should read some things about them, a little dry at times, but I come away with a different perspective with each read). What it may make you realize is this republic is an evolving process and while some seek to throw away things that got us to the table, maybe, just maybe, when our backs are to the wall, we'll come out fightin' to preserve and evolve a little more. In a toast at one of an affair in his honor, George Washington once said, in a toast, "competent powers to Congress for general purposes". I believe the General meant nothing like we have today. I wish us well.

Finally, at this many pages of babbling, I am informed by more than one I must stop.

The words "never" and "always" probably should go away. After all, they are synonymous with….nothing.

'Nite Gracie, or in my case, Karen.

.

www.ingramcontent.com/pod-product-compliance
Lightning Source LLC
Chambersburg PA
CBHW051331170526
45166CB00002B/763